W9-BRQ-261

2

More Grammar Practice

THOMSON

HEINLE

United States • Australia • Canada • Mexico • Singapore • Spain • United Kingdom

Contents

ACC LIBRARY SERVICES
AUSTIN, TX

BASE FORM	-S FORM
I **love** animals.	My mother **loves** children.
We **love** animals.	My father **loves** children.
You **love** animals.	My family **loves** children.
My children **love** animals.	My dog **loves** children.
They **love** animals.	Everyone **loves** children.

LANGUAGE NOTES:

1. Use the –s form after *he, she, it,* singular nouns, *everyone, everybody, everything, someone, somebody, something, no one, nobody, nothing,* or *family.*
2. Add –*es* to verbs that end in *s, sh, tch, ch, x,* or *z:* wash ⟶ washes, touch ⟶ touches.
3. Drop the –*y* and add –*ies* to most verbs that end in *y: try* ⟶ *tries, carry* ⟶ *carries.*
4. Use the base form after *I, you, we, they,* and plural nouns.
5. Three verbs have an irregular –*s* form: *have* ⟶ *has, go* ⟶ *goes, do* ⟶ *does.* The verb *be* has three forms in the simple present tense: (*I*) *am;* (*you, we, they*) *are;* and (*he, she, it*) *is.*

EXERCISE 1 Fill in the blanks with the correct form of the underlined word.

Example: I <u>work</u> in an office. My wife _____ works _____ in a hospital.

1. We <u>write</u> the answers in the workbook. The teacher _____ the questions.

2. I <u>wash</u> the vegetables. My cousin _____ the dishes.

3. My husband <u>speaks</u> Spanish. I _____ Spanish too.

4. I <u>study</u> the newspaper. My sister _____ her schoolbooks.

5. You <u>eat</u> a lot of meat. I _____ a lot of meat too.

6. She <u>cleans</u> the kitchen. He _____ the garage.

7. I <u>enjoy</u> my job. My friend _____ his job too.

8. He <u>lives</u> alone. I _____ with my family.

9. I <u>go</u> to the bank every morning. My husband _____ to the restaurant.

10. My teacher <u>likes</u> the city. I _____ the city too.

11. The bus driver <u>has</u> a nice smile. You _____ a nice smile too.

12. We <u>go</u> to the supermarket on Saturday. He _____ on Thursday night.

13. You <u>walk</u> 2 miles to school. They _____ 1 mile to school.

14. Eggs <u>break</u> easily. A glass _____ easily too.

EXERCISE 2 Fill in the blanks in each paragraph with the words in the box. Each word should be used only one time.

A.

~~own(s)~~	draw(s)	speak(s)
make(s)	write(s)	do(es)	ask(s)

My family works for my uncle. He (**example**) _____*owns*_____ a newspaper. My brother and I are reporters. Every day we (1) _____ questions and (2) _____ news stories. My mother is the cartoonist. She (3) _____ funny pictures of people who are in the news. My father is in charge of advertising. He (4) _____ with companies that want to advertise in our paper. My aunt is the editor-in-chief. She (5) _____ the final decisions about the news stories. My uncle is the managing editor. Everyone (6) _____ what he says.

B.

work(s)	close(s)	come(s)	go(es)
buy(s)	cook(s)	become(s)	open(s)

My husband and I (1) _____ together in a small seafood restaurant. He is the cook. In the morning he (2) _____ to the market and (3) _____ the best fish and vegetables for that day's menu. Then he (4) _____ back to the restaurant and (5) _____ all the foods for the day. We (6) _____ the restaurant at 11:00 a.m., and it quickly (7) _____ very busy. We (8) _____ the restaurant at 10:00 p.m.

C.

work(s)	enjoy(s)	come(s)
tell(s)	bring(s)	examine(s)

My wife is a doctor. All her patients are children. Their parents (1) _____ them to her when they are ill. She (2) _____ them and sometimes gives them medicine. My wife (3) _____ long hours, but she (4) _____ her job. When she (5) _____ home at night, we (6) _____ each other about our day.

PRACTICE 2 Negative Statements with the Simple Present Tense

EXAMPLE	EXPLANATION
My neighbors have two dogs. They **don't have** a cat.	Use *do not* + the base form with *I, you, we, they,* or a plural noun.
My daughter wants a puppy. She **doesn't want** a kitten.	Use *does not* + the base form with *he, she, it,* or a singular noun.

LANGUAGE NOTES:
1. *Don't* is the contraction for *do not. Doesn't* is the contraction for *does not.*
2. Always use the base form after *don't* and *doesn't.*

EXERCISE 1 Write the negative form of the underlined verb.

Example: He talks loudly. We _____don't talk_____ loudly.

1. I swim very well. You _____ very well.

2. He listens to the radio. She _____ to the radio.

3. We grow tomatoes and peppers. They _____vegetables.

4. You know my brother. She _____ my brother.

5. She reads many magazines. We _____ magazines.

6. I watch old TV shows. You _____ old TV shows.

7. They do their laundry. She _____ her laundry.

8. We go shopping at the mall. He _____ shopping.

9. The children stay home. The adults _____ home.

10. He has four brothers. I _____ four brothers.

EXERCISE 2 Rearrange the following words to make correct sentences.

Example: in the west / rise / the sun / doesn't

_____The sun doesn't rise in the west._____

1. a lot of money / have / she / doesn't

_____

2. like / he / to get up early / does / not

_____

3. don't / they / want / a lot of money / to pay

_____

4. she / does / walk to work / not

   _____

5. not / put sugar / in her / does / my mother / tea

   _____

6. rains / every weekend / doesn't / it

   _____

EXERCISE 3 Use a negative verb to complete the answer to each of the following questions.

Example: Why does he walk to work every day?

Because he (not / have) _____*doesn't have*_____ a car.

1. Join me for a cup of coffee?

   No thanks, I (not / drink) _____ coffee.

2. Why don't they laugh at my jokes?

   They (not / like) _____ your sense of humor.

3. You look tired. Are you okay?

   I (not / feel) _____ very well. I think I'll go lie down.

4. Who is that guy driving the red car?

   Sorry, I (not / know) _____ who he is.

5. Why doesn't Miguel come to the restaurant with us?

   He (not / feel) _____ well.

6. Can I borrow her pen?

   Sorry, she (not / have) _____ a pen.

PRACTICE 3 Questions with the Simple Present Tense

WH- WORD	DO / DOES DON'T / DOESN'T	SUBJECT	VERB	COMPLEMENT	SHORT ANSWER
		My friend	has	a dog.	
		She	doesn't have	a cat.	
	Does	she	have	a Labrador?	No, she doesn't.
What kind of dog	does	she	have?		
Why	doesn't	she	have	a cat?	

EXERCISE 1 Rearrange the following words to make questions. Put a question mark at the end of each question.

1. you / your lunch / buy / where / do
   Where do you buy your lunch?

2. ask / do / so many questions / children / why
   _____

3. do / this word / you / how / pronounce
   _____

4. money / we / where / change / do
   _____

5. how often / her e-mail / check / does / she
   _____

6. the children / what flavor / want / do
   _____

7. does / how much / cost / this computer
   _____

8. need / who / to speak to / you / do
   _____

9. he / languages / does / how many / speak
   _____

10. open / do / the banks / when
    _____

EXERCISE 2 Circle the correct word to complete each sentence.

Example: (Does)/ Do he like pizza for lunch?

1. Where / What do you keep the milk?
2. When does / do he eat his dinner?
3. Why don't / doesn't you like your food?
4. Does / Do the baby use a spoon or a fork?
5. Where / What do they want to go?
6. Where do they goes / go for vacation?
7. Do the children wants / want to play now?
8. Where do / does they take vacation?

EXERCISE 3 Write a *yes / no* question for each sentence. Give a short affirmative or negative answer.

Example: She goes to the bank on Monday.

Does she go to the bank on Monday?   No, *she doesn't.*

1. They pay the rent every month.

   _____   No, _____

2. People shake hands to say hello.

   _____   Yes, _____

3. She adds salt to all her food.

   _____   No, _____

4. The car costs a lot of money.

   _____   No, _____

5. He talks to his friend on the phone every night.

   _____   Yes, _____

6. Children like the flavor of spinach.

   _____   No, _____

PRACTICE  4   Uses of the Simple Present Tense

EXAMPLE	USES OF THE SIMPLE PRESENT TENSE
The sun **rises** in the east.	To state a fact
Marianne **comes** from the United States.	To show one's country, city, or place of origin
We **get up** around 6:00 a.m. and go to bed around midnight.	To show a regular activity, a habit, or a custom

EXERCISE 1   Underline the simple present tense verb in each sentence. Then write *fact, origin,* or *custom* beside each sentence, depending on the use of the verb.

Example: Anna <u>comes</u> from Canada.   _origin_

1. The earth circles the sun.   _____
2. I send e-mail every day.   _____
3. Fish come from lakes and oceans.   _____
4. Fruit grows on trees.   _____
5. She gets up at 6:00.   _____
6. She drinks water every day.   _____
7. Elena comes from Russia.   _____
8. The magazine comes once a month.   _____
9. Paper comes from trees.   _____
10. You exercise daily.   _____
11. I go out to eat every Saturday.   _____
12. I speak to my mother every day.   _____
13. Eggs are from chickens.   _____
14. The moon is easy to see at night.   _____
15. The students are from Morocco.   _____
16. He cleans his apartment on Friday.   _____
17. Pollution is from cars.   _____
18. My mother comes from Spain.   _____

EXERCISE 2 Read Marta's schedule and answer each question below.

Name: Marta Vasquez

City, Province, and Country of origin:

Toronto, Ontario, Canada

Activities:

- Jogs—Mondays, Wednesdays, and Fridays
- Plays basketball—Tuesdays and Thursdays
- Goes shopping—Saturdays
- Reads magazines—Sundays

Facts about Marta:

- Tall
- Athletic
- Loves her family
- Two brothers
- One cat

Example: Where does Marta go on Saturdays?

Marta goes shopping on Saturdays.

1. What days does Marta jog?

2. What does Marta do on Tuesdays?

3. What country does Marta come from?

4. How many pets does Marta have?

5. Is Marta short?

6. What does Marta read on Sundays?

7. Does Marta have two sisters?

8. Where in Canada is Marta from?

EXERCISE 3 Write simple present tense sentences about your daily activities and habits.

Example: (in the morning) *I drink orange juice in the morning.*

1. (in the morning) _____

2. (at lunchtime) _____

PRACTICE 5 Frequency Words and Position of Frequency Words

FREQUENCY WORD		EXAMPLE
always	100%	The sun **always** rises in the east.
usually / generally		Children **usually (generally)** like to watch cartoons.
often / frequently		Parents **often (frequently)** read to their children.
sometimes /occasionally		Rivers **sometimes (occasionally)** flood after rain.
rarely / seldom / hardly ever		It **rarely (seldom) (hardly ever)** rains in the desert.
never / not ever	0%	The sun **never** rises in the west.

LANGUAGE NOTES:

1. Frequency words usually come after the verb *be* but before other verbs.
2. The following frequency words can also come at the beginning of a sentence: *usually, generally, often, frequently, sometimes, occasionally. Often, frequently,* and *occasionally* can also come at the end of a sentence.
3. In questions or negative sentences, frequency words usually come before the base verb.
4. Use *how often* in a *wh–* question if the answer is a frequency word or phrase:
   How often do you wash the floor?
   I rarely wash the floor.

EXERCISE 1 Place the frequency words in the sentences.

1. My sister calls me.   (hardly ever)
   My sister hardly ever calls me.

2. My best friend and I eat lunch together.   (frequently)

   _____

3. The banks are open on weekends.   (never)

   _____

4. The post office is closed on holidays.   (always)

   _____

5. We like to go to the park and feed the pigeons.   (occasionally)

   _____

6. I cook dinner, and my roommate washes the dishes.   (often)

   _____

7. He stays up very late the night before an exam.   (generally)

_____

8. The mail comes in the afternoon.   (usually)

_____

EXERCISE **2**   Unscramble the words to write correct statements and questions. If a question mark is provided, make the sentence a question.

1. usually / eat / a big breakfast / I
   *I usually eat a big breakfast*_____.

2. check / you / how often / your voicemail / do

   _____?

3. in the evenings / hardly ever / my roommates / at home / are

   _____.

4. he / out of town on weekends / goes / usually

   _____.

5. the population of the world / how often / double / in size / does

   _____?

6. late / sometimes / is / this bus

   _____.

EXERCISE **3**   Use a frequency word in your answer to each of these questions.

Example: How often do you drink soda?

   *I seldom drink soda.*_____

1. Do you ever go to the beach in December?

   _____

2. How often do your friends call you?

   _____

3. Is the weather here ever cloudy?

   _____

Practice 5   **13**

PRACTICE 6 Contrasting the Simple Present and the Present Continuous Tenses

SIMPLE PRESENT FORM	PRESENT CONTINUOUS FORM
She sometimes **wears** a dress.	She's **wearing** sunglasses now.
She **doesn't wear** shorts.	She **isn't wearing** shorts.
Does she ever **wear** a bathing suit?	**Is** she **wearing** a T-shirt?
No, she **doesn't**.	No, she **isn't**.
How often **does** she **wear** a dress?	What **is** she **wearing?**
Why **doesn't** she ever **wear** a bathing suit?	Why **isn't** she **wearing** shoes?

SIMPLE PRESENT TENSE	EXPLANATION
Plants **need** water in order to live.	Use the simple present tense to talk about a general truth, a habitual activity, or a custom.
We **do** our homework in the evening.	
People **cook** rice in a variety of ways.	

PRESENT CONTINUOUS TENSE	EXPLANATION
They are **studying**.	Use the present continuous tense for an action that is in progress at this moment or for a longer action that is in progress at this general time.
I'm using a grammar workbook in my English class this term.	

EXERCISE 1 Circle all of the simple present verbs. Underline all of the present continuous verbs.

Example: My sister (visits) me on Monday. Today she is visiting friends.

A. (1) My older brother works as a reporter for the largest newspaper in my country. (2) He writes about international news. (3) It is a good job. (4) He and his family move to a new country every year. (5) Right now they're living in Jerusalem. (6) His wife and children are learning Arabic and Hebrew, (7) but my brother knows these languages already. (8) He speaks four languages. (9) He is learning to speak Spanish (10) because he wants to travel in South America.

B. (1) My younger brother is a student. (2) He's studying business at our national university. (3) He works at a couple of part-time jobs during the school year. (4) He likes to try different jobs. (5) Right now he's waiting tables at a restaurant in the evenings. (6) Also, he is managing a car wash on the weekends.

EXERCISE 2 Write the correct form of the verb in each sentence. Choose the simple present or the present continuous verb tense.

Examples: She (like) _____ likes _____ to watch TV at night.

He (talk) _____ is talking _____ on the phone right now.

1. He (sleep) _____ right now. Please call back later.
2. She (type) _____ all of her letters.
3. We (sit) _____ in the best seats for this concert.
4. You (talk) _____ all the time.
5. Please be quiet! I (watch) _____ a good movie.
6. My mother and I (shop) _____ at the mall each month.
7. They (sing) _____ at the concert today.
8. It (rain) _____ right now.
9. Brian (play) _____ soccer with Joe on Tuesday.
10. Susan (wash) _____ her hair every morning.

EXERCISE 3 Fill in the correct missing word for each statement or question in the conversation.

1. **A:** Elaine _____ working on the English homework.
2. **B:** _____ she need help with grammar?
3. **A:** Yes, _____ does.
4. **B:** _____ she having problems with the simple present tense?
5. **A:** No, _____ isn't.
6. **A:** _____ wants to work on reading.
7. **B:** _____ the reading difficult?
8. **A:** Yes, it _____.
9. **A:** She _____ using the dictionary right now.
10. **B:** _____ you want me to help her?
11. **A:** Yes, I _____. Thank you.
12. **B:** No problem. I _____ happy to help Elaine any time.
13. **A:** Do _____ want me to tutor her every Thursday?
14. **B:** No, _____ don't. She usually swims on Thursdays.

PRACTICE 7 Nonaction Verbs

ACTION VERBS	NONACTION VERBS
Carmen **is living** in Osaka, Japan, this year.	She **likes** her new life.
She **is studying** Japanese.	She **doesn't understand** much yet.
	She **hears** some of the words clearly.

LANGUAGE NOTES:

1. We do not usually use the present continuous tense with certain verbs called *nonaction verbs.* These verbs describe a state or a condition, not an action. We use the simple present tense, even when we talk about now.

2. Some nonaction verbs are the following:

be	hear	mean	see
believe	know	need	seem
care	like	own	think
cost	love	prefer	understand
have	matter	remember	want

3. *Think, have,* and the sense perception verbs (*look, taste, feel, smell*) can be both action and nonaction verbs, but the meaning is different.

EXERCISE 1 Underline 20 nonaction verbs in the following diary entry. Some of the verbs will be used more than one time.

Example: I <u>have</u> many letters to write.

Dear Diary,

   I think I really like my life in Japan! I like my host parents, Mr. and Mrs. Yamada. They are very kind to me, and they care for me like a daughter. I like my room, and I love the house. I'm practicing the Japanese language, but I don't yet understand what people are saying in conversations, and I often need my dictionary. I look for many words every day. Sometimes I understand the words, but I don't know what they mean. When Mrs. Yamada suggests that we do something together, I wonder, "Does she want me to do it?" Everything seems so confusing. I need help! Sometimes I prefer to stay in my room because that seems easy. But I believe hard work matters most.

                                                            Carmen

EXERCISE 2 Choose the correct tense from each set of underlined verbs.

Example: He is wanting / (wants) to meet famous movie stars.

Dear Diary,

Life (1) is getting / gets better here in Osaka. My Japanese (2) is improving / improves

every day. I (3) have / am having two new friends, Erika and Satoko, and they

(4) are helping / help me with my language and culture questions. I (5) am wanting / want to

invite them to visit me when I get home to Texas. They (6) are seeming / seem easy to talk

with, and they both (7) are having / have a great sense of humor.

I (8) am liking / like to go shopping. Everything (9) is costing / costs more here, so I

usually just (10) am looking / look at the shop windows. I (11) am hearing / hear a lot of

Japanese conversations when I am in the shops, and I (12) am understanding / understand

about 40 percent of them. I'm a little shy, and I (13) am preferring / prefer just to listen and

not to speak right now. Erika and Satoko sometimes (14) are going / go with me and

(15) are translating / translate for me. I (16) am having / have a good time here.

Carmen

EXERCISE 3 Write a diary entry of your own. Write about your own life and the things that are happening to you now. Use nonaction verbs.

_____

_____

_____

_____

_____

_____

_____

_____

_____

_____

_____

_____

PRACTICE 8 Questions with the Simple Present and the Present Continuous Tenses

WH– WORD	DO or DOES (+N't)	SUBJECT	MAIN VERB	COMPLEMENT
		She	**watches**	TV.
When	**does**	she	**watch**	TV?
		My parents	**speak**	English.
What language	**do**	your parents	**speak?**	
		Your sister	**lives**	with someone.
With whom	**does**	she	**live?**	
Who	**does**	she	**live**	with?
		You	**don't like**	her.
Why	**don't**	you	**like**	her?

QUESTIONS WITH THE PRESENT CONTINUOUS TENSE

WH– WORD	BE (+N't)	SUBJECT	BE	MAIN VERB	COMPLEMENT
		She	**is**	**sitting.**	
Where	**is**	she		**sitting?**	
		You	**aren't**	**listening**	to the music.
Why	**aren't**	you		**listening**	to the music?

EXERCISE 1 Match each question to the correct answer in the second column.

1. Are you speaking to me?
2. Do you want to eat now?
3. What is your name?
4. How long is the movie?
5. When do you go to sleep?
6. How old is she?
7. Is he a doctor?
8. Why is he sleeping?
9. How are you feeling?
10. Am I bothering you?

a. Yumiko Toshimo.
b. At about 11:00 p.m.
c. Yes, I am.
d. Fine, thanks.
e. No, he isn't.
f. Yes, I do.
g. He is tired.
h. Almost 19.
i. No, you're not.
j. About two hours.

EXERCISE 2 Find the mistakes in the underlined portions of the following questions. Rewrite the questions correctly. If there are no mistakes, write *Correct*.

Examples: <u>Is</u> he <u>speak</u> to his parents?

Is he speaking to his parents?

<u>Do</u> you <u>want</u> to come to my house?

Correct

1. <u>Do</u> she <u>visiting</u> her friends in Japan this week?

   _____

2. <u>Are</u> they <u>live</u> in Mexico?

   _____

3. <u>Is</u> she <u>teaching</u> the class today?

   _____

4. <u>Are</u> you <u>wear</u> glasses every day?

   _____

5. <u>Do</u> your mother <u>play</u> the piano?

   _____

EXERCISE 3 Use the words in parentheses to write a question.

Example: I'm not watching TV tonight. (why)

Why aren't you watching TV tonight?

1. Amy is babysitting her little cousin.   (why)

   _____

2. I am traveling soon.   (where)

   _____

3. Steve does his homework.   (when)

   _____

4. We ran 5 miles today.   (with who[m])

   _____

5. They need to go to the dentist.   (why)

   _____

PRACTICE  The Future Tense with *Will*

EXAMPLE	EXPLANATION
People **will live** longer in the future. They **will need** help from their children.	We use *will* + the base form of the verb to make the future tense.
I**'ll be** 75 years old in 2050. You**'ll take** care of your parents.	We can contract *will* with the subject pronouns: *I'll, you'll, he'll, she'll, it'll, we'll, they'll.*
The population **will not** go down. I **won't** live with my children.	To form the negative, put *not* after *will.* The contraction for *will not* is *won't.*

QUESTION FORM	SHORT ANSWER
Will she **live** with her son? Where **will** she **live?** Why **won't** she **live** alone?	Yes, she **will. or** No, she **won't.**

EXERCISE 1 Use the contraction of *will* (*'ll*) with the subject pronouns or *will not* (*won't*) to complete each statement.

Example: (I / not / get on) _____*I won't get on*_____ the bus at 7:30 a.m.

1. (I / call) _____ you when I arrive in the city.

2. (He / not / be) _____ at the bus station.

3. (You / not / need) _____ any money for the taxi.

4. (You / buy) _____ a house one day.

5. (She / meet) _____ you on the street corner.

6. (They / not / like) _____ the menu in the cafeteria.

7. (We / not / go) _____ if it rains tomorrow.

8. (It / be) _____ cloudy in the morning.

9. (It / not / rain) _____ I'm sure.

10. (I / walk) Tomorrow _____ 5 miles.

11. (she / not / play) Tonight _____ basketball.

12. (I / not / look) _____ at my birthday present yet.

13. (He / be) _____ ready for the game.

14. (We / listen) _____ to the music at the concert.

EXERCISE 2 Write questions using *will* and the words in parentheses.

Example: (Why / you / not / be) _____*Why won't you be*_____ there tomorrow?

1. (Where / you / go) _____ to college?
2. (How long / they / study) _____ English?
3. (Why / she / not / finish) _____ that book?
4. (Whom / he / go) _____ to the concert with?
5. (When / we / see) _____ you and your family?
6. (What / you / do) _____ this weekend?
7. (Why / not / you / eat) _____ the fish?
8. (How long / he / try) _____ to get that job?
9. (Where / she / keep) _____ her new dog?
10. (Where / it / be) _____ nice to visit?

EXERCISE 3 Finish the sentences or questions in this conversation using *will* or *won't* plus the verb in parentheses. Use contractions when possible.

Example: *Jane:* (see) _____*I'll see*_____ you when I return to school.

Jane: Hi, John! When [(1) I meet] _____ your family?

John: Sorry, Jane. My family [(2) not / be] _____ here this week. We [(3) not / stay] _____ in the city during our school break. We [(4) rent] _____ a small cabin on a lake for one week. What [(5) you do] _____ during the school break?

Jane: I think [(6) travel] _____ a little. [(7) I not / go] _____ home. My friends and I [(8) try] _____ to rent a car.

John: [(9) be] _____ the car rental _____ expensive?

Jane: I don't think so. We [(10) share] _____ the cost.

John: It sounds like [(11) you have] _____ a great time.

Jane: I hope so. I know [(12) I miss] _____ my family.

John: Have a safe trip, Jane!

EXAMPLE	EXPLANATION
People **are going to live** longer. They **are going to need** help from their children.	We use *be going to* + the base form to form the future tense.
I'm **not** going to live with my children.	To form the negative, put *not* after *am, is, are*.
QUESTION FORM	**SHORT ANSWER**
Is she **going to live** with her son? Where **is** she **going to live**? Why **isn't** she **going to live** with her son?	Yes, she **is**. or No, she **isn't**.

EXERCISE 1 Complete the sentence with the correct form of *be (not) going to* + verb base.

Example: He (go) _____ *is going to go* _____ to school in the fall.

1. Many students (go) _____ to the lecture about politics.

2. Paul (not / study) _____ tonight.

3. Evelyn (not / stay) _____ at home all evening.

4. The phone (be) _____ busy all day tomorrow.

5. The children (play) _____ games at the party.

6. Many men (play) _____ football for the school's team.

7. I (walk) _____ into town.

8. Everybody (sleep) _____ well tonight.

9. She (not / travel) _____ during her vacation.

10. We (not / worry) _____ about our test grades.

EXERCISE 2 Unscramble the following words and phrases. Some sentences are statements. Some are questions.

Example: going to / into a larger apartment / she / is / move

_____ *She is going to move into a larger apartment.* _____

1. finish / you / soon / college / going to / are

   _____.

2. wake up / for class on time / we / going to / are

   _____?

3. I'm / any more money / spend / going to / not

_____.

4. why / eat / lunch with us / going to / you / aren't

_____?

5. this way forever / not / we're / live / going to

_____.

6. going to / in December / they're / to Colombia / move

_____.

7. for a new job / when / going to / you / are / look

_____?

8. he / take / isn't / the exam with us / going to

_____.

EXERCISE 3 Answer the following questions using complete sentences with *be going to*.

Example: Are you going to meet your friends tonight?

Yes, I am going to meet my friends tonight.

1. Where are you going to go after class?

_____

2. When is this term going to be over?

_____

3. What time are you going to go to bed tonight?

_____

4. What are you going to do this weekend?

_____

5. How are you going to use English in your future?

_____

PRACTICE 11 *Will* versus *Be Going To*

USE	WILL	BE GOING TO
Prediction	My father always exercises and eats well. I think he **will live** a long time.	I think my father **is going to live** a long time.
Fact	The sun **will set** at 6:43 tonight. The population **will increase.**	The sun **is going to set** at 6:43 tonight. The population of older **people is going to increase.**
Scheduled Event	The movie **will begin** at eight o'clock.	The movie **is going to begin** at eight o'clock.
Plan	My grandfather **is going to move** to Florida next year.	I **am going to return** to my native country in three years.
Promise	I **will** always take care of you.	
Offer to Help	**A:** This box is heavy. **B:** I'll carry it for you	

EXERCISE 1 Complete the sentences with either *will* or *be going to* along with the verbs in parentheses. In some cases, both are possible.

Example: (go) Tonight I _____*am going to go*_____ to a concert.

1. (smoke) _____ you _____ that cigar in here?

2. (happen) I have a feeling that something good _____ to me today.

3. (see) The doctor _____ you as soon as possible.

4. (meet) We _____ in the library to study for the exam together.

5. (be) _____ you _____ there when I get off the plane?

6. (continue) The stock market _____ probably _____ to be unpredictable for the next few years.

7. (buy) What _____ we _____ him for his birthday?

8. (eat) _____n't you _____ any of this delicious cake?

9. (love) I _____ you forever.

10. (need) You _____ an umbrella today.

11. (give) I _____ you a ride as far as the shopping mall.

12. (be) You _____ sorry if you miss the bus.

13. (graduate) My younger sister _____ from high school.

14. (open) Wait! I _____ the door for you.

15. (go) I _____ to Brazil this summer.

16. (be) I promise I _____ home by midnight.

17. (speak) _____ you _____ with your teacher after class?

18. (meet) "Where are you going?" "I _____ my friend."

19. (send) I _____ you a postcard when I get there!

20. (start) The movie _____ at 8:30.

21. (call) "Antonia called while you were out." "OK, I _____ her back."

22. (cut) "I have decided to cut my hair." "How short _____ it?"

EXERCISE 2 Complete the sentences using *will* for promises or offers to help. Use *be going to* for plans.

Examples: I _____*will*_____ never be impolite.

I _____*am going to*_____ study with Tom tonight.

1. I _____ meet my boss at the train station tomorrow.

2. I _____ mail that letter for you.

3. We _____ move into a larger apartment soon.

4. _____ you marry me?

5. I _____ call you first thing tomorrow.

6. Don't bother shopping. I _____ buy milk on my way home.

7. Dinner _____ be ready in a half hour.

8. We _____ take good care of your children.

9. I liked the movie so much that now I _____ read the book.

10. Next term I _____ work instead of taking classes.

PRACTICE 12 — Simple Past Tense of Regular Verbs

EXAMPLE	EXPLANATION
Martin Luther King, Jr., **lived** in the south. He **organized** peaceful protests.	To make the simple past tense with regular verbs, just add *–ed* or *–d*: Base Forms Past Forms live *lived* organize *organized* carry *carried*
Dr. King **lived** in the south. He **didn't live** in the north.	Use the past form in affirmative statements. Use didn't + the base form in negative statements.
He **wanted to change** certain laws. He **encouraged** people **to protest** bad laws.	The verb after *to* does not use the past form.

LANGUAGE NOTE:

We often use *ago* with the simple past:

I lived there 10 years *ago*.

EXERCISE 1 Underline the verb and rewrite the verb in the simple past tense.

Example: I <u>will cancel</u> my plane reservation.

I canceled my plane reservation.

1. I travel to Peru with my best friends.

_____

2. The workers are painting the walls of the house.

_____

3. The secretary cancels all the doctor's appointments.

_____

4. It rains every day.

_____

5. We live in a crowded city.

_____

6. You will ask for more money at your job.

_____

7. My uncle is going to move on Thursday.

_____

8. The car crashes into the tree.

_____

9. I will wash the dishes in a couple of hours.

_____

10. They hope to be the best students in the class.

_____

11. She carries the baby in her arms.

_____

12. You kick the chair over by mistake.

_____

13. I drop by to say hello.

_____

14. The salesperson is calling to tell us about a new credit card.

_____

15. They are wondering about the price of gasoline.

_____

EXERCISE 2 Each simple past tense sentence has two underlined words but only one mistake. Circle the one mistake and write the correct word on the line.

Example: She <u>needed</u> to (going) home after the party. _____go_____

1. Yesterday, we <u>needing</u> to <u>go</u> to the store for milk and eggs. _____
2. You <u>wanted</u> to <u>buys</u> some candy. _____
3. She <u>tried</u> to <u>helped</u> the woman with her groceries. _____
4. Alberto <u>asked</u> how to <u>finding</u> the vegetables. _____
5. He <u>walked</u> over to <u>seeing</u> the tomatoes and corn. _____
6. I <u>cleans</u> and <u>washed</u> the vegetables from the store. _____
7. They <u>likes</u> to <u>cook</u> vegetables and rice for dinner. _____
8. We <u>stopping</u> to <u>look</u> at the cakes and donuts. _____
9. Ten minutes ago, we <u>waited</u> to <u>finding</u> a parking space. _____
10. You <u>help</u> me to <u>discover</u> a space close to the store. _____

PRACTICE 13 Simple Past Tense of Irregular Verbs

VERBS WITH NO CHANGE IN PAST				FINAL *D* CHANGES TO *T*	
beat	fit	put	spit	bend–bent	send–sent
bet	hit	quit	split	build–built	spend–spent
cost	hurt	set	spread	lend–lent	
cut	let	shut			

VERBS WITH VOWEL CHANGES			
feel–felt	mean–meant*	dig–dug	sting–stung
keep–kept	sleep–slept	hang–hung	strike–struck
leave–left	sweep–swept	spin–spun	swing–swung
lose–lost	weep–wept	stick–stuck	win–won
awake–awoke	speak–spoke	begin–began	sing–sang
break–broke	steal–stole	drink–drank	sink–sank
choose–chose	wake–woke	forbid–forbade	spring–sprang
freeze–froze		ring–rang	swim–swam
		shrink–shrank	
bring–brought	fight–fought	blow–blew	grow–grew
buy–bought	teach–taught	draw–drew	know–knew
		fly–flew	throw–threw
arise–arose	rise–rose	bleed–bled	meet–met
drive–drove	shine–shone	feed–fed	read–read**
ride–rode	write–wrote	flee–fled	
		lead–led	
sell–sold	tell–told	find–found	wind–wound
mistake–mistook	shake–shook	lay–laid	say–said***
take–took		pay–paid	
swear–swore	wear–wore	bite–bit	hide–hid
tear–tore		light–lit	slide–slid
become–became		fall–fell	hold–held
come–came			
eat–ate		run–ran	
give–gave		sit–sat	
forgive–forgave		see–saw	
lie–lay			
forget–forgot	shoot–shot	stand–stood	
get–got		understand–understood	

MISCELLANEOUS CHANGES					
be–was / were	do–did	go–went	have–had	hear–heard	make–made

*There is a change in the vowel sound. *Meant* rhymes with *sent*.

**The past form of *read* is pronounced like the color *red*.

***Said* rhymes with *bed*.

LANGUAGE NOTE:

Use the past form in affirmative statements. Use *didn't* + the base form in negative sentences:
  I *didn't forget* to bring money.

EXERCISE 1 Change the irregular verb to the simple past tense. Some of the statements are negative. Rewrite the complete sentence with a past tense expression.

Examples: The house (shake) in the wind. *The house shook in the wind.*

  The building (not / shake). *The building didn't shake.*

1. I (not / leave) the house at 7:45 a.m.

   _____

2. She (speak) to the class for two hours.

   _____

3. He (teach) us how to speak with an excellent accent.

   _____

4. We (not / write) in our journals last night.

   _____

5. The boys (win) the prize for best spellers.

   _____

6. The girls (swim) in the ocean all day.

   _____

7. The teachers (not / meet) on Wednesday afternoon.

   _____

8. I (not / do) any of my homework because I was sick.

   _____

9. The tourists (not / go) on the bus tour yesterday.

   _____

10. The policeman (come) to the scene of the accident.

    _____

11. Sorry! We (eat) all of the pizza.

    _____

12. She (have) a lot of patience to finish the math problems.

    _____

PRACTICE 14 Negatives and Questions with the Simple Past Tense

WH- WORD	DID / DIDN'T	SUBJECT	VERB	COMPLEMENT	SHORT ANSWER
		My friend	**had**	good grades.	
		She	**didn't have**	bad grades.	
	Did	she	**have**	good grades last year?	No, she **didn't.**
Where	**did**	she	**go**	to school?	
Why	**didn't**	she	**have**	good grades last year?	

EXAMPLE	EXPLANATION
The student **didn't succeed.** They **weren't** able to sleep well.	Use *didn't* + the base form in negative statements. Use *wasn't* and *weren't* for *be* negative statements.
Why **did** the students **succeed?** **Did** they take the same test? **Were** any students unhappy?	Questions use *did* (or sometimes *didn't*) and the base form of the verb. *Be* questions use *was* and *were*.

 **EXERCISE 1** Ask a question in response to each sentence. Use the time words in parentheses.

Examples: He passes the test every week.   (last week)

Did he pass the test last week?

He wasn't happy.   (not / yesterday)

Wasn't he happy yesterday?

1. The child feels sick today.   (yesterday)

   _____

2. She is dizzy and tired.   (yesterday afternoon)

   _____

3. She sleeps 10 hours every night.   (last night)

   _____

4. The doctors are worried about the child.   (not / this past week)

   _____

5. They find hospital rooms for their patients.   (not / this morning)

   _____

6. The child is in bed now.   (not / a few minutes ago)

_____

7. Her father makes her eat some soup.   (a few hours ago)

_____

8. She drinks some herbal tea.   (not / a little while ago)

_____

EXERCISE 2   Answer each question about yourself.

Example: Did you go to Paris last year?

_____No, I didn't go to Paris._____   or   _____Yes, I went last year._____

1. Where did you go yesterday?

_____

2. How did you get there?

_____

3. Did you ever fly anywhere?

_____

4. Whom did you ride with on your trip?

_____

5. Were you a student three years ago?

_____

6. When did you buy this book?

_____

7. Did you catch a cold this year?

_____

8. How long did you watch TV last night?

_____

EXERCISE 3   Write four questions in the simple past tense for your teacher or your boss.

Example: _____Did you drive to work today?_____   or   _____Weren't you busy last night?_____

1. _____
2. _____
3. _____
4. _____

PRACTICE 15 Subject and Object Pronouns

EXAMPLE	EXPLANATION
Greta loves music. Yesterday, **she** bought five new CDs.	We use subject pronouns to take the place of subject nouns.
She also bought a CD player. She bought **it** for a good price.	We use object pronouns to take the place of object nouns.
She got some CDs for her boyfriend. She bought them **for him.**	An object pronoun can follow a preposition.

LANGUAGE NOTES:

1. We use pronouns to take the place of nouns.
2. The object pronouns are *me, you, him, her, it, us,* and *them.* Compare subject and object pronouns.

		Examples:		
Subject Pronouns	**Object Pronouns**	**S**	**V**	**O**
I	me	You	see	me.
you	you	I	see	you.
he	him	She	sees	him.
she	her	He	sees	her.
it	it	I	see	it.
we	us	They	see	us.
they	them	We	see	them.

EXERCISE 1 Fill in each blank with a subject or an object pronoun.

Example: What are flea markets?

_____*They*_____ are markets where you can buy almost anything second-hand.

People who go to flea markets are looking for bargains. They often find

(1) _____. My aunt met her husband at a flea market.

He sold (2) _____ some second-hand jewelry.

(3) _____ wasn't very expensive. Then he asked

(4) _____to have a cup of tea with (5) _____. Now he

teases (6) _____ by saying that she was the best bargain

(7) _____ ever found. She tells (8) _____ that he

should have looked for a better deal.

EXERCISE 2 Unscramble the following words to make correct sentences.

Example: French / I / you / helped / learn

I helped you learn French.

1. to me / she / on the phone / talked

   _____

2. we / ice cream / them / bought

   _____

3. loves / she / him / very much

   _____

4. want / him / to / I / to talk

   _____

5. he / a stereo / wants / for us / to buy

   _____

6. them / I / don't / know / very well

   _____

7. to listen / he / her / wants

   _____

8. I / like / tennis / play / to / her / with

   _____

9. yesterday / the present / gave /him / she

   _____

10. asked / we / about it / her

    _____

EXERCISE 3 Write a sentence using each pair of pronouns given.

Example: (them / you) _You gave them a beautiful gift._

1. (she / me) _____

2. (him / I) _____

3. (us / they) _____

4. (we / you) _____

PRACTICE 16 Possessive Forms of Nouns

We use possessive pronouns to show ownership or relationship.

NOUN	ENDING	EXAMPLES
Singular noun: *cat*	Add apostrophe + *s.*	I put food in the **cat's** dish.
Plural noun ending in *–s:* *boys*	Add apostrophe only.	Open the windows in the **boys'** room.
Irregular plural noun: *children*	Add apostrophe + *s.*	Open the windows in the **children's** room.
Names that end in *–s:* *Charles*	Add apostrophe only *or* Add apostrophe + *s.*	This is **Charles'** cousin. This is **Charles's** cousin.

LANGUAGE NOTES:

1. We use the possessive forms for people and other living things:
   I borrowed my *sister's* car.   *Julia's* friend is from Colombia.
2. For inanimate objects, we usually use "the _____ of _____":
   We usually use the door *at the back of the house.*
3. We can use a possessive adjective and a possessive noun together:
   Could you give me *your boss's* phone number?
4. We can use possessive adjectives to show possession. Possessive adjectives are *my, your, his, her, its, our,* and *their.*
   I'm wearing *my* coat. That's *your* bag.

EXERCISE 1 Fill in the blanks with the correct possessive form.

Example: My wife *'s*_____ cooking is even better than my mother *'s*_____ cooking.

1. Stop! That's James _____ toothbrush.
2. Can you get me Ms. Reese _____ e-mail address?
3. Football players _____ uniforms are very hard to get clean.
4. Your company _____ new Web site is really well designed.
5. Other companies _____ Web sites aren't nearly so attractive.
6. You'll find the dresses you want in the girls _____ department.
7. You should go to the children _____ shoe department.
8. Women _____ clothing is on the fourth floor.
9. Go to the third floor for men _____ clothing.

10. Children! Don't pull the cat _____ tail!

11. She's wearing her grandmother _____ diamond bracelet.

12. Everyone wants to go to John _____ party Saturday night.

13. Quick, hide the cake! I hear Daddy _____ footsteps!

14. Let me take a look at my boss _____ schedule.

15. Wait a minute. This isn't Dr. Williams _____ signature.

16. Our book club is reading my favorite author _____ latest book.

17. Show us that picture of your family _____ new house.

18. The hurricane washed away many families _____ houses.

19. I can't read my teacher _____ handwriting.

20. What are the political parties _____ the United States?

EXERCISE 2 Use the words to write a sentence that contains a possessive form. (The words are not always in the correct order.)

Example: the table / the leg / is broken

The leg of the table is broken.

1. where is / wallet / Papa

2. he is wearing / shirt / Dan

3. someone tore / cover/ the book

4. the chair / the arm / is broken

5. what is / this car / the price

6. cap /the pen / missing

WHOSE + NOUN	AUXILIARY VERB	SUBJECT	VERB	ANSWER
Whose dress	did	she	borrow?	She borrowed her *sister's* dress.
Whose pen	can	I	use?	You can use *my* pen.
Whose sister	is	that?		That is *his* sister.

LANGUAGE NOTE:

Whose + a noun asks a question about possession.

EXERCISE 1 Write a follow-up question with *whose* for each statement given.

Example: **A:** I found someone's books in the library.

         B: *Whose books did you find in the library?*

1. **A:** We picked up a stray cat on the way home.

 B: _____

2. **A:** Someone's book was left in the back seat of the car.

 B: _____

3. **A:** I want to try someone's dessert recipe.

 B: _____

4. **A:** She should take my advice.

 B: _____

5. **A:** The teacher corrected someone's homework.

 B: _____

6. **A:** They went to their friends' house.

 B: _____

7. **A:** The robbers used someone's key to enter the house.

 B: _____

8. **A:** The police discovered someone's jewelry in a paper bag.

 B: _____

9. **A:** Someone's composition will win the award.

 B: _____

10. **A:** Someone's dog is wandering around in the street.

 B: _____

11. **A:** It's chasing someone's cat.

    B: _____

12. **A:** The cat is climbing up someone's tree.

    B: _____

EXERCISE **2**   Write questions about the nouns in each sentence. Begin each question with *Whose*.

Example: What a beautiful car.

       Whose car is it? _____

1. That's not your umbrella.

   _____

2. You got an invitation to a party?

   _____

3. I don't recognize this coat.

   _____

4. This isn't my medicine in the medicine cabinet.

   _____

5. Look at this mess!

   _____

6. I found this camera.

   _____

PRACTICE 18 Possessive Adjectives and Pronouns

EXAMPLE	EXPLANATION
That is **my** book. **Our** apartment is small.	The possessive adjective must come before a noun. We can't use it alone or without a noun.
That book is **mine**. (mine = my book) That apartment is **ours**.	The possessive pronoun takes place of a noun. It never comes before a noun.

LANGUAGE NOTES:

1. Be careful with *his* and *her*.

   I have a married *brother*. *His* wife is very nice.

   The *bride* looks beautiful. *Her* father looks proud.

2. When we use a possessive pronoun, we omit the noun. Compare:

   Her dress is white. ⟶ *Your* dress is blue. **or** *Yours* is blue.

3. Compare subject pronouns, possessive adjectives, and possessive pronouns:

Subject Pronouns	Possessive Adjectives	Possessive Pronouns
I	my	mine
you	your	yours
he	his	his
she	her	hers
it	its	—
we	our	ours
they	their	theirs

EXERCISE 1 For each underlined pair, choose the correct possessive form.

Example: Put your / yours coat on. It's cold outside!

1. This bag is not mine. I think it's <u>your / yours</u>.

2. She is a doctor. <u>Her / Hers</u> sister is a lawyer.

3. Is this mine or <u>your / yours</u>?

4. That's his office. It's not <u>my / mine</u>.

5. I don't know <u>their / theirs</u> address.

6. I think that house is <u>their / theirs</u>.

7. This table is our / ours.

8. Your / Yours tape recorder is broken. Why don't you borrow my / mine?

9. Our / Ours car is white. They / Theirs is red.

10. Her / Hers hair is the same length as my / mine.

11. Do you want me to take yours / your picture?

12. His mother is from my / mine native country.

13. She took our / ours umbrella and now she thinks it's her / hers.

14. Please don't take my / mine textbook without my / mine permission.

15. Their / Theirs children are coming over with their / theirs friends.

16. This isn't her / hers scarf. Her / Hers is blue.

17. Our / Ours vacation was as good as your / yours.

18. They went to the restaurant with their / theirs friends and my / mine.

EXERCISE 2 Rewrite each sentence below, replacing the underlined portion with a correct possessive pronoun or possessive adjective.

Example: This is a picture of John and Anne's new baby.

This is a picture of their new baby.

1. The boys' clothes are in the washing machine.

   _____

2. That suitcase isn't your suitcase.

   _____

3. The little girl's kitten ran away.

   _____

4. The next day the kitten returned to the little girl's family's house.

   _____

5. My pen ran out of ink, so I'm going to use your pen.

   _____

6. She announced that Jim's flight would arrive early.

   _____

7. Jeanne's flight arrived earlier than our flight.

   _____

PRACTICE 19 Questions about the Subject

WH– WORD	DO / DOES / DID	SUBJECT	VERB	COMPLEMENT
What	does	The bride she She Who	throws throw? throws caught	something. the bouquet. the bouquet?
What	did	The guests they Some guests How many guests	brought bring? brought brought	something. gifts. gifts?
Why	do	Some women they Which women	try try try	to catch the bouquet. to catch the bouquet? to catch the bouquet?
		Something What	happened happened	next. next?

LANGUAGE NOTES:

1. Questions about the subject are different from other questions. They don't include *do, does,* or *did.*
2. We usually answer a subject question with a subject and an auxiliary verb:
   Who caught the bouquet?   The bride's cousin *did.*
3. What happened is a subject question. We usually answer with a different verb:
   What happened after the wedding?   The bride and groom *went* on a honeymoon.
4. After *who,* use the *-s* form for the simple present tense. After *how many,* use the base form. After other questions, use the *-s* form or the base form, depending on whether the noun is singular or plural:
   Who has the prettiest dress?   *Which girl was* the bridesmaid?
   How many people *want* to dance?   *Which girls were* the nicest?

EXERCISE 1 Write a question about the subject of each sentence.

Example: *Who sent you the information by e-mail?*

My brother sent me the information by e-mail.

1. _____

   Answer: Tommy wrote the answers on the palm of his hand.

2. _____

   Answer: Two police officers caught the robbers.

3. _____

   Answer: Jorge usually brings his sister.

4. _____

   Answer: The <u>climbers</u> always carry first-aid equipment.

5. _____

   Answer: <u>Chang</u> took everyone to dinner.

6. _____

   Answer: The <u>volcano</u> destroyed several villages.

7. _____

   Answer: <u>Our</u> ship survived the tsunami.

8. _____

   Answer: My grandparents are coming to see <u>us.</u>

9. _____

   Answer: <u>Five</u> firefighters fought the fire.

10. _____

    Answer: The <u>mailcarrier</u> brought the mail.

11. _____

    Answer: The <u>Italian</u> woman sang the song.

12. _____

    Answer: The <u>ship</u> sank.

EXERCISE 2 Choose the best response for each question.

Example: Who met her at the train station?

      (a. Her father did.)   b. Her father did meet.

1. What broke the window?

    a. A baseball did.   b. A baseball did break.

2. Who ate my strawberries?

    a. I do.   b. I did.

3. What caused the accident?

    a. A speeding driver did.   b. A speeding driver did cause the accident.

4. Who told you?

    a. She.   b. She did.

PRACTICE 20 Forms and Uses of Reflexive Pronouns

SUBJECT	VERB	REFLEXIVE PRONOUN
I	see	myself.
You	see	yourself.
He	sees	himself.
She	sees	herself.
It	sees	itself.
We	see	ourselves.
You	see	yourselves.
They	see	themselves.

EXAMPLE	EXPLANATION
Sylvia sometimes blames **herself.** (DO) I tell **myself** that he loves me. (IO) Be good to **yourself.** (OP)	A reflexive pronoun can be a direct object (DO), an indirect object (IO), or the object of a preposition (OP).
She hates to eat **by herself.** She has to do everything **all by herself.**	We often add *all by* before the reflexive pronoun to mean *alone*.

LANGUAGE NOTES:

1. If the subject and object are the same, we use a reflexive pronoun as the object.
2. After an imperative, use *yourself* or *yourselves* depending on whether *you* refers to one person or more:
   You singular: Get *yourself* a lawyer.
   You plural: Get *yourselves* a lawyer.

EXERCISE 1 Write the correct reflexive pronoun in the blank.

Example: She gave _____*herself*_____ a party.

1. We sang _____ a song.

2. The old man drew _____ a map.

3. The bird saw _____ in the mirror.

4. He is in love with _____.

5. It's so loud. I can't hear _____ think.

6. If you're hungry, make _____ a sandwich.

7. We gave _____ a pat on the back.

8. He gave _____ a headache worrying about the situation.

9. Don't drive _____ crazy trying to solve this problem.

10. Can you teach _____ vocabulary?

11. If the alarm doesn't work, you'll have to wake _____ up.

12. I go home every night and make _____ some dinner.

13. They can't earn enough money to support _____.

14. Look, that man over there is talking to _____.

15. She ate the whole cake, and she made _____ sick.

16. Babies can't feed _____.

17. We saved our money until we had enough to buy _____ a boat.

18. Dennis hurt _____ with the electric drill.

EXERCISE 2 Circle the best reflexive pronoun for each item.

Example: His problem is that he doesn't have any confidence in (himself)/ herself.

1. You'll have to turn the key in the ignition. The car won't start itself / yourself.

2. She didn't know anyone in the class, so she introduced themselves / herself to the person next to her.

3. For the next three months the students prepared themself / themselves for the exam.

4. The older sister told her sister ghost stories until she even frightened herself / themselves.

5. Don't let that little boy play with that knife. He'll cut himself / themselves.

6. No one invited us to the party, so we invited ourself / ourselves.

7. They attacked me, so I had to defend ourselves / myself.

8. People would enjoy talking with you more if you didn't feel so sorry for themselves / yourself.

9. Other people won't believe in you if you don't believe in yourself / themselves.

10. If all of you start saving money now, you'll thank ourselves / yourselves in 20 years.

11. At the end of the dinner we excused ourselves / ourself.

12. He promised themselves / himself that he would never lie to his parents again.

13. If you want to understand another person, try putting yourself / himself in his place.

14. It's good for people to be able to laugh at theirselves / themselves now and then.

REGULAR NOUN PLURALS

WORD ENDINGS	SINGULAR NOUNS	PLURAL ADDITIONS	PLURAL FORMS
Vowel	bee, banana	+ *s*	bees, bananas
s, ss, sh, ch, x, z	dish, watch	+ *es*	dishes, watches
Voiceless consonants	cat, lip	+ *s*	cats, lips
Voiced consonants	card, pin	+ *s*	cards, pins
Vowel + *y*	boy, day	+ *s*	boys, days
Consonant + *y*	lady, story	*y* + *ies*	ladies, stories
Vowel + *o*	video, radio	+ *s*	videos, radios
Consonant + *o* *Exceptions:* photos, pianos, solos, altos, sopranos, autos, avocados	potato, hero	+ *es**	potatoes, heroes
f or *fe* ***Exceptions:* beliefs, chiefs, roofs, cliffs, chefs, sheriffs	leaf, knife	*f* + *ves***	leaves, knives

IRREGULAR NOUN PLURALS

SINGULAR	PLURAL	EXAMPLE	EXPLANATION
woman foot goose	women feet geese	Men and women came to America from many countries.	Vowel change.
sheep fish	sheep fish	He caught six fish for dinner.	No change.
child person	children people	Many people came to the celebration.	Different word form.
	pajamas, pants scissors	Those pants are clean.	No singular form.
news politics		The news is not good.	Singular form ends in -*s*. No plural form.

EXERCISE 1 Circle the correct form of the underlined noun or pronoun.

Example: When I was a (kid)/ kids, we always had to wash the dish /(dishes) after dinner.

1. We took a couple of sandwiches / sandwichs with us for lunch.

2. Dress the baby in his pajama / pajamas and put him to bed.

3. A few basketball players are 7 <u>feet / foot</u> tall.

4. Ranchers who raise <u>sheeps / sheep</u> have both wool and meat.

5. Most of the news <u>seems / seem</u> to be bad.

6. During the rain all of the <u>seates / seats / seat</u> in the stadium got wet.

7. I washed my jeans and <u>it / they</u> shrank so much that I can't get <u>it / them</u> on.

8. Could you get me two <u>boxes / boxs</u> of animal crackers at the store?

9. The <u>chiefs / chieves</u> spoke to their own people about the new laws.

10. You should wash your <u>glasses / glasss</u> because they're so dirty you can't see anything.

11. The hunters came back with three <u>deer / deers.</u>

12. Let's get a couple of new <u>suitcases / suitcase</u> for our trip.

13. We'll remember that day all our <u>lives / lifes.</u>

14. This paper is going to take me at least three more <u>hours / houres.</u>

15. In the town square is a monument to the <u>heroes / heros</u> of the revolution.

16. In the spring new <u>leafs / leaves</u> appear on the trees.

17. The <u>man's / men's</u> restroom is on the right, just beyond the newsstand.

18. You can buy <u>dictionaries / dictionarys</u> in both book form and electronic form.

19. The police came as soon as <u>he / they</u> could.

20. All cultures have their own <u>believes / beliefs.</u>

21. Take this CD player to a store that fixes <u>stereoes / stereos.</u>

22. Your scissors are so sharp that <u>they / it</u> cut me.

23. The <u>roofs / rooves</u> of the buildings were covered with snow.

24. Tropical <u>fish / fishes</u> are popular for saltwater aquariums.

25. Passengers are not allowed to play <u>radios / radioes</u> during the flight.

26. After your <u>classes / class</u> are over, you can go home.

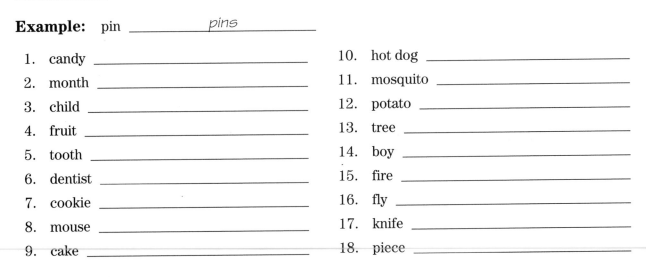

EXERCISE 2 Write the plural form of each regular or irregular noun.

Example: pin _____*pins*_____

1. candy _____

2. month _____

3. child _____

4. fruit _____

5. tooth _____

6. dentist _____

7. cookie _____

8. mouse _____

9. cake _____

10. hot dog _____

11. mosquito _____

12. potato _____

13. tree _____

14. boy _____

15. fire _____

16. fly _____

17. knife _____

18. piece _____

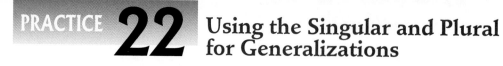

PRACTICE 22 Using the Singular and Plural for Generalizations

EXAMPLE			EXPLANATION
A child	needs love.		When we make a generalization, we say that something is true of the noun in general.
Children	need love.		
A big city	has	a lot of traffic.	To make a generalization, we use a singular noun after *a*, or *an*, or the plural noun with no article.
Big cities	have	a lot of traffic.	

LANGUAGE NOTES:

1. We use the singular form of *hundred, million,* etc. to talk about an exact number:
   I invited *a hundred* people to my wedding.
2. We use the plural form of *hundreds, millions,* etc. to talk about inexact numbers.
   Hundreds of people attended the soccer match.
3. After *every* and *each*, we use a singular noun. After *all* we use a plural noun.

EXERCISE 1 Decide if each expression is *specific* or *general*. Write your decision on the line.

Example: Children _____ *general* _____   The child _____ *specific* _____

1. the geese _____
2. geese _____
3. ten geese _____
4. a goose _____
5. every mother _____
6. each person _____
7. one thousand drivers _____
8. hundreds of cooks _____
9. all working people _____
10. an emotion _____
11. the emotion _____
12. emotions _____
13. two emotions _____
14. each pilot _____
15. all students _____

EXERCISE 2 Decide if the sentence is a generalization or a specific statement. Circle the best answer.

Example: (A vegetarian)/ The vegetarian is someone who doesn't eat meat.

1. A vegetarian / The vegetarian refused to eat the chicken we offered her.
2. The exercise / An exercise helps you understand generalizations.
3. Exercises / The exercises give students a lot of practice!
4. I love children / the children.
5. The children / Children in my neighborhood are very well behaved.
6. Every child / children should learn a second language.
7. All of the person / people voted for her.
8. She spent about two hundred dollars / hundreds of dollars on that table.
9. That city has a problem with crime / the crime.
10. Crime / The crime was committed at midnight.
11. Women / The women are more expressive than men / the men.
12. Life / The life can be difficult.
13. Life / The life of a fruit fly is short.
14. There are exactly four thousand / thousands of seats in the auditorium.
15. History / The history is an interesting subject.
16. I like to study history / the history of my country.
17. Did you ask all of the student / students to come to the play?
18. You should eat vegetables / the vegetables every day.

EXERCISE 3 Write sentences including the following subjects in the specific or general form.

Example: teachers (general) _Teachers want the best for their students._

teachers (specific) _The teachers at the college worked at night._

1. politician (specific)

   _____

2. politician (general)

   _____

3. hundreds of people (general)

   _____

4. one hundred people (specific)

   _____

PRACTICE 23 — Noncount Nouns

These are some ways that we can distinguish count and noncount nouns:

Group A. Nouns that have no distinct, separate parts. We look at the whole:

milk	wine	poultry	meat	thunder	electricity
oil	yogurt	soup	butter	cholesterol	lightning
water	pork	bread	paper	blood	air

Group B. Nouns that have parts that are too small or insignificant to count:

rice	salt	hair	grass	sand
sugar	popcorn	snow	corn	

Group C. Nouns that are classes or categories of things. The members of the category are not the same:

money or cash (nickels, dimes, dollars)   fruit (cherries, apples, grapes)
food (vegetables, meat, spaghetti)   makeup (lipstick, rouge, eye shadow)
furniture (chairs, tables, beds)   homework (compositions, exercises)
clothing (sweaters, pants, dresses)   jewelry (necklaces, bracelets, rings)
mail (letters, packages, postcards, fliers)

Group D. Nouns that are abstractions:

love	happiness	nutrition	music	information
life	education	intelligence	art	nature
time	experience	unemployment	work	help
truth	crime	pollution	health	noise
beauty	advice	patience	trouble	energy
luck	knowledge	poverty	fun	friendship

Group E. Subjects of study:

history	grammar	biology
chemistry	geometry	math (mathematics)
English	Spanish	political science

LANGUAGE NOTE: Some nouns can be used as count nouns in some cases and as noncount nouns in other cases.

Examples: I washed my *hair*.   I found a *hair* in my soup.

EXERCISE 1 These are some things that people can buy at a grocery store. Write *count* or *noncount* next to each word.

1. candy _____
2. onion _____
3. bread _____
4. oil _____
5. flour _____
6. pickle _____

7. soy sauce _____
8. toothpaste _____
9. toothbrush _____
10. sugar _____
11. banana _____
12. rice _____

EXERCISE 2 Choose the best form of the underlined word.

People who want to stay healthy and slim should watch what they eat.

Example: (Food)/ Foods with a lot of (1) butter / butters can make a person obese and can harm the heart. (2) Sugar / Sugars makes a person gain weight too. Eating a lot of (3) rice / rices, (4) noodle / noodles, or (5) bread / breads can make a person gain weight as well. As we all know, too much (6) coffee / coffees or (7) tea / teas makes a person nervous, and too much (8) alcohol / alcohols can lead to alcoholism.

People with (9) food / foods allergies must also be careful of what they eat. Some people can't eat (10) wheat / wheats, so they can't eat (11) bread / breads or (12) noodle / noodles that are made from (13) wheat / wheats. Others are allergic to milk (14) product / products, so they can't drink (15) milk / milks or eat (16) cheese / cheeses or (17) ice cream / ice creams. If a person is very allergic to a (18) food / foods, eating it can endanger his or her (19) life / lives.

(20) Knowledges / Knowledge about food can save your life.

EXERCISE 3 Choose the correct form of the underlined words.

Example: His (hair)/ hairs is thick and straight.

1. The police found two blond hair / hairs on the victim's coat.
2. Some restaurants use napkins that are made of paper / papers.
3. We have to write three paper / papers for this class.
4. My grandparents lived long and happy life / lives.
5. Sometimes life / lives can be very hard.
6. Pour the juice into a glass / glass.
7. This mirror is made of a glass / glass.
8. Time / Times goes by very quickly.
9. She called me five time / times yesterday.
10. It was an experience / experiences I will always remember.

PRACTICE 24 Quantities with Noncount Nouns

These are some ways that we can measure count and noncount nouns.

BY CONTAINER	BY PORTION	BY MEASUREMENT	BY SHAPE / WHOLE PIECE	OTHER
a bottle of water	a slice or piece of bread	an ounce of sugar	a loaf of bread	a piece of mail
a carton of milk	a piece of meat	a quart of oil	an ear of corn	a piece of furniture
a jar of pickles	a piece of cake		a piece of fruit	a piece of advice
a can of soda	a strip of bacon	a pound of meat	a head of lettuce	a piece of information
a cup of yogurt	a bowl of soup		a roll of film	
a glass of water	a piece or sheet of paper	a gallon of milk	a candy bar	a work of art
a bag of flour			a tube of toothpaste	a homework assignment
a box of paper clips	a slice of pizza	a pint of cream	a bar of soap	
	a scoop of ice cream			

EXERCISE 1 The following quantities are not correct. Change the container or portion to the amount you buy at the supermarket or cook with at home.

Example: a jar of cake   _a piece of cake_

1. a bottle of cereal   _____

2. a jar of soap   _____

3. a bag of jam   _____

4. a box of milk   _____

5. a can of butter   _____

6. a bar of sugar   _____

7. a stick of flour   _____

8. a loaf of chocolate   _____

9. a teaspoon of candy   _____

10. a carton of beans   _____

EXERCISE 2 Use the nouns in the box to fill in the blanks in the conversation between Monica and Stephen as they plan their shopping trip.

Example: I need to buy two heads of _____lettuce_____ for the salad.

cereal	beans	flour	margarine	toothpaste
bread	milk	meat	gas	mayonnaise

Monica: Let's go shopping for groceries. If you'll check the pantry, I'll make a list.

Stephen: Okay. Let's see. We need (1) a can of _____, (2) a box of _____, (3) a quart of _____, and (4) a pound of _____.

Monica: Anything else?

Stephen: Yes, I need (5) a bag of _____ and (6) a stick of _____ for the cake I'm going to make tonight.

Monica: Good. I need (7) a tube of _____. How about you? Do you need anything else?

Stephen: Maybe (8) a loaf of _____ and (9) a jar of _____ for sandwiches. I think that's all.

Monica: Great. Let's go to the store.

Stephen: Oh, don't let me forget that we also need to put (10) a few gallons of _____ in the car.

EXERCISE 3 Think about the items in your kitchen at home. List them with quantity expressions.

Example: _a can of tomatoes_

a bag of oranges

In my kitchen at home, I have:

1. _____
2. _____
3. _____

PRACTICE 25 — *There + a Form of Be*

	THERE	*BE*	ARTICLE / QUANTITY	NOUN	PLACE OR TIME
Count	There	will be	a	ball game	at 2:00 p.m. tomorrow.
	There	are	two	sandwiches	in the refrigerator.
Noncount	There	was	some good	news	on the front page.
	There	is	no	water	on the moon.

LANGUAGE NOTE:

Observe the word order in questions with *there*:

    Is there life on Mars? No, there probably isn't.

    Are there any messages for me? Yes, there are.

    How many messages *are there*? There are four.

EXERCISE 1   Write *There is* or *There are* before each article or quantity + noun.

Example: _____There is_____ a large school next to my apartment.

1. _____ a great selection of CDs at the mall.
2. _____ several shoe stores next to the music store.
3. _____ delicious popcorn at the movie theater.
4. _____ no homework tonight.
5. _____ a small red car in the parking lot.
6. _____ some vegetables and noodles in my soup.
7. _____ two computers for sale.
8. _____ no fish in this soup.
9. _____ some lemonade on the table.
10. _____ many happy students in this class.

EXERCISE 2   Write *Is there / Are there / Was there / Were there* before each question.

Example: _____Was there_____ a party last night?

1. _____ other students in the library yesterday?
2. _____ any good movies out right now?
3. _____ a medical emergency last week?
4. _____ any children in the park an hour ago?
5. _____ someone in the hallway?

6. _____ anything to eat?

7. _____ time at the end of yesterday's test?

8. _____ any phone messages?

9. _____ any e-mails yesterday afternoon?

10. _____ a teacher in that classroom?

EXERCISE 3 Fill in the blanks with nouns from the box. Use each noun only once.

furniture	information	election	children	picture
meat	credit cards	onions	schedule	

Example: Is there any _____ *meat* _____ on my sandwich?

1. Are there any _____ on my sandwich?

2. How many homeless _____ are there in this city?

3. There's some good _____ on the bulletin board.

4. There's an _____ for the presidency every four years.

5. There are two _____ in my wallet.

6. There's a _____ of my family in my wallet.

7. There's a _____ of today's movies in the newspaper.

8. Is there any _____ in the apartment?

EXERCISE 4 Unscramble the words to make sentences with *there*.

Example: the swimming pool / are / two girls / in / there

There are two girls in the swimming pool. _____

1. are / on my desk / there / a phone / and a lamp

_____

2. there / many ducks / were / on the pond

_____

3. was / at the college / a great professor / there

_____

4. this morning / was / about the weather / there / bad news

_____

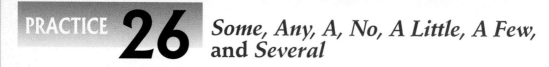

PRACTICE 26 — Some, Any, A, No, A Little, A Few, and Several

	SINGULAR COUNT	PLURAL COUNT	NONCOUNT
Affirmative	There's **a** clock in the kitchen.	There are (**some**) windows in the kitchen.	There's (**some**) rice in the kitchen.
		I have (**a few**) questions.	I need (**a little**) help.
		I have (**several**) mistakes on my composition.	I need (**a little**) more time.
Negative	There isn't **a** clock in the kitchen.	There's **no** clock in the kitchen.	There isn't (**any**) rice in the kitchen
		There aren't (**any**) windows in the kitchen.	There's **no** rice in the kitchen.
		There are **no** windows in the kitchen.	
Question	Is there **a** clock in the kitchen?	Are there (**any**) windows in the kitchen?	Is there (**any**) rice in the kitchen?

LANGUAGE NOTES:

1. *An* is used before singular count nouns that begin with a vowel:
   I have *an* uncle, *an* aunt, and *a* grandmother.
2. *Some* and *any* can also be used in questions and alone.
   Do you have *some* change? Do they need *any*?
3. Use an affirmative verb before *no*. Don't use the indefinite article after *no*:
   There is *no* time.
   There is *no* answer to your question.
   There *isn't any* time.
   There *isn't an* answer to your question.

EXERCISE 1 Fill in each blank with *some, any, a, an,* or *no*.

Example: Do you have _____*any*_____ money? I forgot my wallet today.

A. Do you have (1) _____ milk that we could borrow? We had (2) _____ yesterday, but we drank it all. Now we don't have (3) _____, and we need (4) _____ for the baby's breakfast.

B. If we're going to the swimming pool, let's take (1) _____ suntan lotion. I like the kind with (2) _____ high sunscreen level. I won't buy it if it doesn't have (3) _____ sunscreen.

C. Your problem is that you don't get (1) _____ exercise. You ought to go on (2) _____ healthy diet and do (3) _____ exercises every day.

D. I can't go with you to the movies tonight because I have to write

(1) _____ composition for one of my classes. In fact, I have

(2) _____ homework for every class. I can't believe you don't have

(3) _____ homework. You're really lucky!

EXERCISE **2**   Carol is going to make Fabulous Fish Soup. She has crossed out the ingredients that she doesn't need. Make two lists below: the things she doesn't need (use *any* or *a / an* when listing each of these items) and the things she has to buy at the store (use *some* or *a / an* when listing each of these items).

<table>
<tr><td colspan="3" align="center">Fabulous Fish Soup</td></tr>
<tr><td>¼ cup olive oil</td><td>2 yellow onions</td><td>1 can of tomato sauce</td></tr>
<tr><td>1 potato</td><td>1 large carrot</td><td>salt and pepper</td></tr>
<tr><td>2 teaspoons parsley</td><td>2 bay leaves</td><td>6 tablespoons butter</td></tr>
<tr><td>2 medium turnips</td><td>4 cups fish broth</td><td>3 pounds fish steaks</td></tr>
<tr><td>2 teaspoons flour</td><td></td><td></td></tr>
</table>

Carol doesn't need:

Example: _____ any olive oil _____

1. _____
2. _____
3. _____
4. _____
5. _____

Carol needs:

Example: _____ some parsley _____

1. _____
2. _____
3. _____
4. _____
5. _____
6. _____

PRACTICE **27** *A Lot of, Much, Many*

	PLURAL COUNT	NONCOUNT
Affirmative	He has **many** friends. He has **a lot of** friends.	He has **a lot of** time.
Negative	He doesn't have **many** friends. He doesn't have **a lot of** friends.	He doesn't have **much** time. He doesn't have **a lot of** money.
Question	Does he have **many** friends? Does he have **a lot of** friends? How **many** friends does he have?	Does he have **much** time? Does he have **a lot of** time? How **much** time does he have?

A Lot of = Large Quantity. No Problem Is Presented.	*Too Many / Too Much* = Excessive Quantity. A Problem Is Presented.
A **lot of** students study at the library. (**Many** students study at the library. They don't finish **much** work.) I have **a lot of** homework. I have **a lot of** cousins.	**Too many** students study at the library. The library is crowded and noisy. I don't have time to talk to you. I have **too much** homework. I have no time to study. I have **too many** family responsibilities.

LANGUAGE NOTES:

1. *Much* is rarely used in affirmative statements. It is more common to use *a lot of* in affirmative statements.
2. *A lot of* has a neutral tone. It shows a large quantity but doesn't present a problem. *Too much* or *too many* usually presents a problem or a complaint.
3. Use *too much* with noncount nouns. Use *too many* with count nouns.

EXERCISE 1 Circle the correct underlined word or words in each sentence.

Example: She can't eat many / (much) sugar.

1. Don't eat <u>too much / too many</u> oil or fat.

2. The body needs <u>a lot of / a little</u> fat in the diet.

3. A year ago, he ate <u>too much / too many</u> rice and bread.

4. It is good to eat <u>much / many</u> vegetables every day.

5. We don't have <u>much / several</u> soda for everyone.

6. Can you buy <u>several / a little</u> cans of soda for me?

7. Do you eat <u>much / many</u> sugar?

8. Does he eat <u>many / much</u> cookies?

9. I have <u>a little</u> / <u>a few</u> friends with children.

10. If you're taking the kids to the beach, take <u>a little</u> / <u>several</u> towels with you.

11. The kids always have <u>little</u> / <u>a lot of</u> fun at the beach.

12. Children always say "Give us just <u>a few</u> / <u>a little</u> more time."

13. Their grandmother gave them <u>a few</u> / <u>a little</u> money for a snack.

14. They bought <u>several</u> / <u>a little</u> chocolate bars with the money.

EXERCISE 2 Write *problem* when something excessive or bad is stated. Write *no problem* on the line when no problem is presented.

Example: A few of my friends live near your house. _____*no problem*_____

1. I read a lot of books for school. _____

2. I spend too much time on the computer. _____

3. You have several international friends. _____

4. You have too many homework assignments. _____

5. We work too much. _____

6. We have many assignments. _____

7. She has a few beauty secrets for nice skin. _____

8. She rests a lot. _____

9. She drinks a lot of water. _____

10. That costs a lot of money. _____

11. There are too many clouds today. _____

12. They don't need to lose a few pounds. _____

EXERCISE 3 Write a paragraph about your hometown. Use the quantity phrases *a lot of, much, many, a little, a few,* and *several* to describe what your hometown has and doesn't have.

Example: My hometown doesn't have much crime.

_____

_____

_____

_____

_____

_____

PRACTICE 28 Adjectives

EXAMPLE	EXPLANATION
We ate a **big** meal. I don't like to eat **fatty** foods.	An adjective describes a noun. An adjective can come before a noun.
Fast food is **inexpensive.** Models are **thin.** You look **healthy.** Burgers taste **delicious.**	An adjective can come after the verb *be* and the sense-perception verbs: *look, seem, sound, smell, taste, feel.*
Are you **concerned** about your weight? I'm **tired** after work. The health club is **located** near my house.	Some *–ed words* are adjectives, such as: *tired, worried, crowded, located, married, divorced, excited, disappointed, finished, frightened.*
He did exercises and **got tired.** I ran for 3 miles and **got thirsty.** If you eat too much candy, you're going to **get sick.**	An adjective can follow *get* in these expressions: *get tired, get worried, get hungry, get sleepy, get thirsty, get married, get divorced, get sick, get angry.* In these expressions, *get* means *become.*

LANGUAGE NOTES:

1. We do not make adjectives plural:
   a *thin* model   *thin* models   a *big* glass   *big* glasses
2. *Very, quite,* and *extremely* can come before adjectives.
   You are *very* healthy.   They are *extremely* tired.

EXERCISE 1 Underline the adjective in each sentence or question.

Example: That man seems <u>angry</u>.

1. We like to eat salad from a wooden bowl.
2. I love your dress! Is it expensive?
3. That television is heavy.
4. My married sister lives a few miles from here.
5. After the hike, they got thirsty.
6. The blue glass holds water.
7. We made the cake from sweet butter.
8. I got sick before my assignment ended.
9. Why are you worried about your test?
10. She was frightened by the dark.

EXERCISE 2 Write one or more appropriate adjectives after each sense-perception verb below.

Example: Your hair looks _____beautiful_____. Did you have it cut?

1. After running the marathon, I felt _____.

2. The river water felt _____ on his bare feet.

3. My cooking tastes _____.

4. Ice cream tastes _____.

5. This milk smells _____. Let's throw it out.

6. Your soup smells _____. What did you put in it?

7. The sky looks _____. I think it's going to rain.

8. Mother looks _____. Let's make dinner for her.

9. Learning a new language seems _____, but it isn't really.

10. He seems _____. Did he have a bad day?

EXERCISE 3 Circle the best adjective to complete the sentence about a good vacation experience.

1. I had fun! I took a boring / wonderful vacation last summer.

2. I was excited / disappointed to leave on vacation.

3. I felt disappointed / tired that I could take only a week's break.

4. I flew to a tropical / arctic island with my bathing suit packed.

5. I spent most of my time on the sunny / cloudy beaches.

6. I got thirsty / angry on the hot beach.

7. One afternoon I met a dull / pleasant woman.

8. She said that she liked undercooked / gourmet food.

9. She told me that her uncle owned a famous / awful restaurant.

10. She invited me to go there with her for a delicious / disgusting meal.

11. The restaurant was crowded / empty.

12. A busy / nervous waiter took our order.

PRACTICE 29 Noun Modifiers

EXAMPLE	EXPLANATION
Do you have an **exercise machine?** A **farm worker** gets a lot of exercise. Some people eat at a **fast-food restaurant.** I joined a **health club.**	A noun can modify (describe) another noun. The second noun is more general than the first. *Strawberry jam* is a jam. A *shoe store* is a store.
I bought new **running shoes.** Do you ever use the **swimming pool?**	Sometimes a gerund describes a noun. It shows the purpose of the noun.
My five-**year-old** son prefers candy to fruit. **Potato chips** have a lot of grease. My new shoes are in the **shoebox.**	The first noun is always singular. A *five-year-old* son is a son who is five *years* old.
Do you have your **driver's license?** I can't understand the **owner's manual** for my new VCR.	Sometimes a possessive form describes a noun.

LANGUAGE NOTE:
Some noun modifiers become attached to the noun: *shoe + box = shoebox*, *book + store = bookstore*. These are called *compound nouns*.

EXERCISE 1 Answer each question, using one of the nouns in the question as a noun modifier in your answer. If the word is singular, use an article.

Example: What kind of store can you buy shoes at? _____ *a shoe store* _____

1. What kind of government runs a city? _____

   _____

2. In what kind of class do you study biology? _____

   _____

3. What kind of food do you give to cats? _____

   _____

4. At what kind of place do you wash cars? _____

   _____

5. What kind of doctor takes care of your eyes? _____

   _____

6. What kind of camera do you use to take videos? _____

   _____

7. What kind of sale do stores have in the summer? _____

_____

8. What kind of a belt keeps you safe in a car? _____

_____

9. What do we call a person who stars in movies? _____

_____

10. In what kind of garden do people grow vegetables? _____

_____

11. What kind of salad has fruit in it? _____

_____

12. What do you call a burger with cheese? _____

_____

13. What do you call a mine where people dig for diamonds? _____

_____

14. What do you call a store that has different kinds of departments? _____

_____

15. What do you call a book full of telephone numbers? _____

_____

16. What do you call a machine that you can use to send faxes? _____

_____

17. What do you call a sale that people have in their garage? _____

_____

18. What do you call a child who is 10 years old? _____

_____

EXERCISE 2 Match the first noun (the noun modifier) with the second (the "main" noun).

Example: bed ——————————— room

1.	credit	a.	table
2.	living	b.	ball
3.	tea	c.	boots
4.	feather	d.	water
5.	grammar	e.	card
6.	book	f.	pillow
7.	kitchen	g.	book
8.	base	h.	room
9.	rubber	i.	cup
10.	tap	j.	bag

EXAMPLE	EXPLANATION
I choose my food **carefully.** Some people eat **poorly.**	An adverb of manner tells how or in what way a person does something. We form most adverbs of manner by putting –*ly* at the end of an adjective.
Do you eat **well?**	The adverb for *good* is *well.*
He worked **hard** and came home **late.** Don't eat so **fast.**	Some adverbs of manner do not end in –*ly.* The adjective and the adverb are the same.

LANGUAGE NOTES:

1. *Hard* and *hardly* are both adverbs, but they have completely different meanings.
   He worked *hard.* = He put a lot of effort into his work.
   He *hardly* worked. = He did very little work.
2. An adverb of manner usually follows the verb phrase.
   She ate her lunch *quickly.*
   You speak English *well.*
3. *Very, extremely,* and *quite* can come before an adverb.
   They work *very* slowly.
   She drives *extremely* well.
   You speak *quite* clearly.

EXERCISE 1 Change the following adjectives to adverbs of manner.

Example: quick _____ *quickly* _____

1. dangerous

   _____

2. normal

   _____

3. safe

   _____

4. rapid

   _____

5. fast

   _____

6. constant

   _____

7. slow

   _____

8. good

   _____

EXERCISE 2 Circle the adjective in each statement. Change the adjective to an adverb and write it on the line. Some adjectives and adverbs have the same form.

Example: I ate my food (quick) _____ *quickly* _____

1. I finished the work easy. _____
2. They sold the house cheap. _____
3. She waited for you patient. _____
4. I didn't tie the rope secure. _____
5. I want to pronounce words correct. _____
6. He held the baby careful. _____
7. I didn't arrive late. _____
8. Make sure you eat slow. _____
9. They studied hard last night. _____
10. She hard studied and failed the test. _____
11. You need to speak soft. _____
12. They don't celebrate birthdays happy. _____
13. The teacher speaks well about her students. _____

EXERCISE 3 Insert *very, quite,* or *extremely* before each adverb.

Example: She studied ^very hard for the test.

1. She spoke Chinese fluently.

2. He pushed his friend roughly.

3. I'm sorry I completed my work carelessly.

4. They walked into the classroom quietly.

5. Honestly, I am upset about the decision.

6. We completed our project thoughtfully.

7. You politely asked me to wait with you.

8. The cat moves silently in the night.

PRACTICE **31** Adjectives versus Adverbs

ADJECTIVE	ADVERB
Jim looks **serious**. (*Serious* describes Jim.)	Jim is looking at his mistakes **seriously**. (*Seriously* tells how he is looking at his mistakes.)
The music sounds **good**. (*Good* describes the music.)	The singer sings **well**. (*Well* describes the singing.)
Your composition looks **good**. (Good describes the composition.)	You wrote it **well**. (Well describes how you wrote it.)
My father got **angry**. (Angry describes my father.)	He spoke **angrily** to his children. (Angrily tells how he spoke.)

LANGUAGE NOTES:

1. An adjective describes a noun: (*happy* baby). An adverb describes a verb or verb phrase: (walked *slowly*), *an adjective:* (*well* known), or another adverb: (*very* slowly).
2. Use an adjective after the following verbs if you are describing the subject. Use an adverb if you are telling how the action (the verb) is done:

   smell   sound   seem   feel   taste   look   appear

   She *looks happy.*   She *is looking* at the contract *carefully.*
3. Use an adjective, not an adverb, in expressions with *get* or *become:*

   I got *cold* and *wet* in the rain.

EXERCISE 1 Choose the correct adjective or adverb for each sentence.

1. My sister is a <u>wonderful / wonderfully</u> cook.

   _____

2. She cooks extremely <u>good / well</u>.

   _____

3. Her Italian dishes taste particularly <u>good / well</u>.

   _____

4. She got <u>excitedly / excited</u> when she saw her sister get off the airplane.

   _____

5. They talked <u>excited / excitedly</u> until late into the night.

   _____

6. You seem particularly <u>happy / happily</u> today.

   _____

7. He became <u>rich / richly</u> from his Internet company.

   _____

8. My teacher is <u>fluent / fluently</u> in three languages.

_____

9. He and his wife dance <u>graceful / gracefully</u> together.

_____

10. My husband took me to a <u>romantic / romantically</u> movie.

_____

EXERCISE 2 Find the mistake in the underlined portion of each sentence. Rewrite the sentence correctly. If there are no mistakes in the sentence, write *correct*.

Example: My father drives very <u>careful</u>.

My father drives very carefully. _____

1. He is a very <u>careful</u> driver.

_____

2. I lost the race because I ran <u>slow</u>.

_____

3. Sorry I'm late! My watch is <u>slow</u>.

_____

4. He visits his parents in Brazil <u>frequent</u>.

_____

5. That perfume smells <u>beautifully</u>.

_____

6. If you don't dress <u>quick</u>, we will be late.

_____

7. The customer got <u>angrily</u> when the salesperson ignored him.

_____

8. He spoke <u>seriously</u> to his children.

_____

PRACTICE 32 *Too and Enough*

TOO + ADJECTIVE / ADVERB TOO + MUCH / MANY + NOUN	ADJECTIVE / ADVERB + ENOUGH	ENOUGH + NOUN
I'm **too tired** to exercise.	A diet of colas and burgers is not **good enough.**	Children don't get **enough exercise.**
It's never **too late** to change your habits.	I walked **quickly enough** to raise my heart rate.	I don't have **enough time** to exercise.
Children eat **too much food** that is high in calories.		
They spend **too many hours** in front of the TV.		

LANGUAGE NOTES:

1. *Too* indicates a problem. The problem is stated or implied.
2. Put *too* before the adjective or the adverb: *too old, too tired, too slowly.*
3. Use *too much* before noncount nouns and *too many* before plural count nouns:

   too much time   too many calories   too much grease   too many sodas
4. *Enough* means as much or as many as needed. Put *enough* after the adjective or adverb. Put *enough* before the noun:

   old enough, tall enough, slowly enough

   enough money, enough time, enough books
5. An infinitive phrase (*to* + a base verb) can follow a phrase with *too* and *enough*:

   He's too young *to understand* life.

   You're old enough *to drive.*

EXERCISE 1 Write *too, too much,* or *too many* before each word.

Example: _____*too*_____ loud

1. _____ boxes
2. _____ small
3. _____ long
4. _____ information
5. _____ hot
6. _____ expensive
7. _____ sugar
8. _____ slowly
9. _____ ice
10. _____ carefully
11. _____ tired
12. _____ thin
13. _____ problems
14. _____ heavy
15. _____ difficult
16. _____ simply
17. _____ fish
18. _____ money
19. _____ hard
20. _____ people

EXERCISE 2 Write *enough* before or after each word. If there are two possibilities, write both of them.

Example: Is the classroom _____ quiet ____*enough*____ to study?

1. Are there _____ sandwiches _____?

2. Are the children _____ big _____ to go to camp?

3. Did I cut the string _____ short _____?

4. You gave me _____ advice _____.

5. Is it _____ cold _____ for you?

6. We think that car is _____ cheap _____.

7. The cook put _____ salt _____ in the soup.

8. She ran _____ quickly _____ to win the road race.

9. I think there is _____ hot water _____ for a shower.

10. They had _____ hope _____ to try calling again.

11. Are you _____ tired _____ to sleep well tonight?

12. They drive _____ carefully _____ at night.

13. Are there _____ books _____ on Brazilian history?

14. We believe there is _____ light _____ to see.

15. The exercise is _____ easy _____ to finish.

16. There is _____ meat _____ for the whole family to eat.

17. The hotel manager gave us _____ towels.

18. Are there _____ forks _____ on the table for 6 people?

EXERCISE 3 Read each question. Write an answer using *enough, too, too much,* or *too many*.

Example: Why are you tired?

I didn't sleep enough last night. _____

1. Why aren't you hungry?

   _____

2. Why are you exercising so much?

   _____

PRACTICE 33 *Too* and *Very*

SUBJECT	VERB	*VERY / TOO*	ADJECTIVE OR ADVERB
That computer	is	**very**	expensive, but I've saved enough to buy it.
That computer	is	**too**	expensive for me to buy.
I	was	**very**	tired, but I went to work.
I	was	**too**	tired to exercise after work.
She	speaks	**very**	quickly.
You	speak	**too**	quickly. I can't understand you.

LANGUAGE NOTE:

Don't confuse *very* and *too. Too* always indicates a problem in a specific situation. The problem can be stated or implied. *Very* is a neutral word.

EXERCISE 1 Match the comments of speaker A on the left with the responses of speaker B on the right.

Speaker A

1. Why can't he vote? _____*i*_____
2. How old is her son? _____
3. What's the weather like outside? _____
4. Why don't you want to plant a garden this weekend? _____
5. Why can't we get this bookcase into the truck? _____
6. What do you like best about this flower? _____
7. Why are you leaving so early in the morning? _____
8. Shall we hike to the top of the mountain? _____
9. Why are you staying at work so late tonight? _____
10. Are you coming with me to a movie? _____

Speaker B

a. It smells very sweet.

b. No, I'm too busy.

c. It's very far.

d. He's very young.

e. It's too tall.

f. It's too wet.

g. It's very hot today.

h. No, it's too far.

i. He's too young.

j. I'm very busy.

EXERCISE 2 Fill in the blanks with *too* or *very.*

Example: I won't let my daughter wear makeup because she's _____*too*_____ young.

1. I can't keep up with you. You're walking _____ fast.
2. The dress is _____ beautiful. I think I'll buy it.
3. That box is _____ heavy for me to lift.
4. The belt is _____ big for me. It's falling off.
5. She speaks _____ slowly so we can understand everything.

6. It's _____ cold out today. Make sure you wear a coat.

7. It's _____ hot to wear a coat today.

8. It's _____ late to call them. They're probably asleep.

9. She's _____ short to be a professional model.

10. Her hair is _____ long, and she wants to grow it even longer.

11. I'm _____ full, but I can still eat dessert!

12. They are _____ shy to speak in public.

EXERCISE 3 Finish each sentence, using *too* or *very* + an adjective. Choose one adjective from the box.

sour	sick	difficult	angry	sad
hot	old-fashioned	tight	sunny	easy
lumpy	dirty	boring	cloudy	valuable	tired

Example: I'm going to bed early tonight. I'm _____*very tired*_____.

1. Pass me the sugar, please. This lemonade is _____.

2. After the operation the man got better, but he was still _____.

3. When I told my boss about my mistake, she was _____.

4. I didn't finish the homework because it was _____.

5. Let's go cheer Jane up. She looks _____.

6. Let your soup cool off a minute. It's _____.

7. Could you bring me a larger size? These shoes are _____.

8. Your mother wouldn't like this style. She's _____.

9. This weather is perfect for a picnic! It's _____.

10. I finished the exam in just 20 minutes. It was _____.

11. He doesn't sleep well on that bed. It's _____.

12. Please be careful when you wash that vase. It is _____.

13. Don't bring that dog into the house! He's _____.

14. I went to sleep during the movie. It was _____.

15. They didn't go swimming at the beach. It was _____.

PRACTICE 34 — *For, In, During, By, and Ago*

TIME WORD	EXAMPLE	EXPLANATION
for	He spoke on the phone **for** an hour.	*For* tells how long.
in	I finished the job **in** May, 2000.	Use *in* with a specific year or month.
	I finished the job **in** five days.	Use *in* to mean after or within a period of time.
during	We visited the Eiffel Tower **during** our trip to Paris.	Use *during* with an activity.
by	You must renew your passport **by** July of next year.	*By* means no later than.
ago	We moved into this house three years **ago**.	*Ago* means before now.

LANGUAGE NOTES:

1. Compare *before* and *ago:*
   She got married *before* she graduated.
   She got married three years *ago.*
2. Compare *during* and *for:*
   She fell asleep *during* the movie.
   She slept *for* two hours.
3. Compare *after* and *in:*
   I'll come back *in* an hour.
   I'll come back *after* I go to the post office.
4. Compare *before* and *by:*
   I have to return my library books *before* Friday. (Friday is not included.)
   I have to return my library books *by* Friday. (Friday is included.)

EXERCISE 1 Fill in each blank with *during* or *for*.

Example: I was asleep _____*during*_____ the movie.

1. We discussed our plans _____ our lunch break.
2. Something woke her up _____ the night.
3. They drove _____ 13 hours before they stopped for the night.
4. Your name came up _____ our conversation.
5. The astronauts remained in orbit _____ 41 days.
6. It rains a lot here _____ the winter months.
7. If you feel dizzy, sit down _____ a few minutes.
8. _____ the war, he fought in many battles but was never wounded.

9. I think you should stay in bed _____ a few days.

10. The children become restless _____ long car trips.

EXERCISE 2 Fill in each blank with *ago* or *in*.

Example: I learned to do the job _____ *in* _____ five days.

1. We love to visit the public gardens _____ the spring.

2. The twins were born four years _____.

3. You'd better hurry. The plane leaves _____ 30 minutes.

4. A few days _____ she got a telephone call that changed her life.

5. I always do my best work _____ the morning.

6. Your plane left five minutes _____. You're too late.

7. What did you just say a few minutes _____?

8. Why don't we travel somewhere together _____ August?

9. My brother left home two years _____, but he often visits us.

10. I'll get back to you _____ just a minute.

EXERCISE 3 Fill in each blank with *by* or *in*.

Example: He will lose five pounds _____ *by* _____ October.

1. She has to be at her desk _____ 8:00 each morning.

2. I will complete my homework _____ three hours.

3. My brother caught the flu, but _____ one week he got better.

4. If you'll help me, we can finish _____ noon.

5. _____ a few hours, they will leave.

6. Everyone had left the birthday party _____ 7:00 p.m.

7. Fortunately the rain had stopped _____ the time I left the building.

8. Many of the runners ran the race _____ 20 minutes.

9. You have to be back to school _____ Monday.

10. _____ January, I return to China.

PRACTICE # 35 The Past Continuous Tense

EXAMPLE	EXPLANATION
Last night at midnight I **was watching** the late show on TV. My roommates **were watching** it with me.	To form the past continuous tense, we use *was* or *were* + verb–*ing*: I, he, she, it ⟶ *was* you, we, they ⟶ *were*
I **wasn't sleeping.** My roommates **weren't paying** attention.	To form the negative, put *not* after *was* or *were*. The contraction for *was not* is *wasn't*. The contraction for *were not* is *weren't*.
Was he **living** in the United States? Yes, he **was**. **Where was** he **living**? **Who** was **living** in Germany?	Question formation: *Yes / no* question and short answer *Wh–* *Wh–* subject

EXERCISE 1 Fill in the past continuous form of the verb given to tell about events that were happening around the world yesterday.

Example: (rain) It _____was raining_____ in the Nile River valley.

1. (snow) It _____ in the Himalayan Mountains.

2. (try) People _____ to climb Mount Everest.

3. (care) Nurses _____ for patients.

4. (enter) New babies _____ the world.

5. (smile) Their parents _____.

6. (take) Students _____ university entrance exams.

7. (tell) A camper _____ a story to her friends around a campfire.

8. (think) A young man in Thailand _____ about his sweetheart.

9. (wonder) His sweetheart _____ if he loved her.

10. (break) In the Antarctic an iceberg _____ free.

11. (discover) An astronomer _____ a new star in a distant galaxy.

12. (worry) A mother in Nigeria _____ about her son.

13. (plan) A famous chef _____ a dinner for the King of Morocco.

14. (win) A baseball team _____ a game for the first time in three years.

15. (enjoy) A Russian journalist _____ his vacation in Odessa.

16. (apply) A teacher in Brazil _____ for graduate school.

17. (plow) A farmer in the Philippines _____ his field.

EXERCISE 2 Unscramble the words and phrases to make each past continuous question.

Example: speaking to / who / she / on the phone / was

Who was she speaking to on the phone?

1. were / to my advice / listening / you

    _____

2. to the music / they / how long / listening / were

    _____

3. playing / was / where / last night / the guitar / he

    _____

4. was / who / with him / singing

    _____

5. in the afternoon / he / reading / a book / wasn't

    _____

6. watching / the new TV show / were / the children / when

    _____

7. rude / being /weren't / to the customers / we

    _____

8. was / she / after work / what / yesterday / doing

    _____

EXERCISE 3 Write sentences about what you and your friends _were_ or _weren't_ (_was / wasn't_) doing last night.

Example: _I wasn't exercising last night._

1. (my friends / study English)

    _____

2. (I / speak on the phone)

    _____

3. (I / write a letter)

    _____

4. (my friends/ cook a big dinner)

    _____

Uses of the Past Continuous Tense

EXAMPLE	EXPLANATION
What **were** you **doing** at 10:00 a.m. yesterday? I **was working** in the computer lab.	We use the past continuous tense to show what was in progress at a specific moment in the past.
The cashier **was counting** the money when the robbers **entered** the store. While the robbers **were holding** her up, the cashier secretly **pushed** an alarm button.	We use the past continuous tense with the simple past tense to show the relationship of a longer past action to a shorter past action.

LANGUAGE NOTES:

1. You can show the relationship of a longer past action to a shorter past action in two ways:
   - Use *when* + the simple past tense with the shorter action.
     The cashier was counting the money *when* the robbers *entered* the store.
   - Use *while* + the past continuous tense with the longer action.
     While the robbers *were holding* her up, the cashier secretly pushed an alarm button.
2. If the time clause precedes the main clause, separate the two clauses with a comma.

MAIN CLAUSE	TIME CLAUSE
He was living in the city	when he died.

TIME CLAUSE	MAIN CLAUSE
When he died,	he was living in the city.

EXERCISE 1 Use a past continuous or simple past verb to complete each sentence when you rewrite each sentence. Check each sentence for correct comma use.

Example: (while / I / walk) it started to rain

While I was walking, it started to rain.

1. I was working on the computer (when / the electricity / go off).

   _____

2. Another car hit mine (while / I / stop) at the red light.

   _____

3. (while / my sister / have) a party, my cousins came to visit.

   _____

4. (while / he / ski) on the mountain, he broke his leg.

   _____

5. The telephone rang (while / we / eat) dinner.

   _____

6. We found a lot of wildflowers (while / we / hike).

    _____

7. (when / you / come over), I was watching a video tape.

    _____

8. She was working at the clothing store (when / you / see) her for the first time.

    _____

9. (when / you / call) me on the phone, the children were talking loudly.

    _____

10. I read my book (while / the children / sleep).

    _____

11. He fell off the horse (while / he / ride) across the field.

    _____

12. (when / I / arrive) at the doctor's, many patients were waiting.

    _____

EXERCISE 2 Answer the question about *what you did* or *what you were doing.*
Use the simple past or the past continuous.

Example: While I was preparing my dinner, *my husband helped me chop vegetables.*

1. When it started to rain, I _____
2. While I was eating dinner, I _____
3. When my friend came to visit, I _____
4. While my friends were studying, I _____
5. When I went to the bank, I _____
6. While I was cleaning my kitchen, _____
7. When I wrote you a letter, _____
8. While I was doing the laundry, _____

PRACTICE 37 *Was / Were Going To*

WAS / WERE GOING TO (THE PLAN)	BUT. . . (WHY THE PLAN DIDN'T HAPPEN)
We **were going to** come to see you,	but our car broke down.
He **was going to** give her the good news,	but somebody else told her first.

LANGUAGE NOTES:

We use *was / were going to* + the base form of the verb to describe a plan that we didn't carry out. It means the same thing as *was / were planning to* + the verb.

EXERCISE 1 Complete each sentence with the missing word or verb.

Example: We were _____*going to*_____ to meet you yesterday, but our car broke down.

1. He _____ going to call you, but he had a lot of homework.

2. You were going to _____ your homework, but you forgot.

3. They _____ going to study for the exam, but they lost their notebooks.

4. It was _____ to be sunny today, but it is terrible out.

5. We were going _____ pay that bill, but we lost it in all our papers.

6. She was going to go to the dentist, but _____ didn't have enough money.

7. I _____ going to write that letter, but I continued to forget.

8. We were going to tell you about that, _____ we were a little nervous.

9. They were going _____ save dessert for you, but they ate the last piece.

10. _____ was going to bring lunch for both of us, but he left it on the bus.

11. She _____ going to clean my room, but she ran out of time.

12. You were going _____ water the plants, but you fed the cat first.

EXERCISE 2 Complete each of the following sentences with a plan expressed with *was / were going to.*

Example: _I was going to buy you a present_ , but I didn't have enough money.

1. _____ , but you interrupted me.
2. _____ , but it started to rain.
3. _____ , but I wasn't strong enough.
4. _____ , but my parents wouldn't let me.
5. _____ , but I had too much to do.
6. _____ , but I changed my mind.
7. _____ , but the dog ate it.
8. _____ , but my boss asked me to do something else instead.
9. _____ , but I just wasn't hungry enough.
10. _____ , but just then the phone rang.
11. _____ , but it was too hot.
12. _____ , but my friends wanted to go home instead.
13. _____ , but it was easier to do it by e-mail.
14. _____ , but I forgot.

EXERCISE 3 Write a complete sentence responding to each of the items below with *was / were going to but . . . .*

Example: You didn't mail these bills.

I was going to mail them, but the post office was closed.

1. You didn't meet me at the train station.

_____

2. You never told me you had an accident with the car.

_____

3. Why didn't you buy a gift for the bride and groom?

_____

4. You didn't pay your credit card bill.

_____

5. You didn't make a doctor's appointment.

_____

PRACTICE **38** Overview of Modals and Related Expressions

LIST OF MODALS	FACTS ABOUT MODALS

can
 	
could
 	
should
 	
will
 	
would
 	
may
 	
might
 	
must
	1. The base form follows a modal. Never use an infinitive after a modal.
	    You **must pay** your rent. (*Not:* You must to pay your rent.)
	
	2. Modals never have an *–s*, *–ed*, or *–ing* ending.
	    He **can** go. (*Not:* He cans go.)
	
	3. To form the negative, put *not* after the modal.
	    You **should not** leave now.
	
	4. You can make a negative contraction with some modals:
	    can't couldn't shouldn't won't wouldn't mustn't
	
	5. Some verbs are like modals in meaning: *have to, had better, ought to, be able to, be supposed to, be permitted to, be allowed to:*
	    He **must** sign the lease. = He **has to** sign the lease.

EXERCISE 1 Read the following statements and underline the modals and verbs that act as modals. (See item 5 in the box above.)

Example: In some countries, people <u>are supposed to</u> keep dogs on leashes.

1. Humans can train dogs to do tricks.

2. The successful dog trainer has to keep several things in mind.

3. A proverb says "You can't teach an old dog new tricks."

4. While this proverb may not always be true, it is certainly easier to train a puppy than an adult dog.

5. First, you must develop a good relationship with the puppy.

6. Next you have to make sure that the puppy understands what you want it to do.

7. Of course, the puppy should not be permitted to run wild.

8. Dogs can't concentrate on one task for a long time.

9. A young dog ought to be able to learn to sit up, roll over, shake hands, and fetch a stick.

10. A trainer should praise the dog when it performs a trick correctly.

11. Soon it ought to understand the trick when you say "Sit up" or "Fetch."

12. Some dogs will learn faster than others, of course.

13. You shouldn't punish your dog if it can't learn quickly.

14. You must try to figure out what the problem is.

15. You might come to the conclusion that your dog just isn't a performer.

16. Both you and your pet will be happier if the dog is permitted to be itself.

17. Children might like the responsibility of a pet.

18. Older children are able to train dogs to do simple tricks.

19. They may be allowed to feed, groom, and walk the dog.

20. A dog might be the right choice for a family pet.

EXERCISE 2 Circle the correctly formed modal in each sentence.

Example: He willn't / (won't) help train the dog.

1. Humans can training / train dogs to do tricks.

2. The successful dog trainer must / has keep several things in mind.

3. You can't / can't to teach an old dog new tricks.

4. This proverb mays / may not always be true.

5. You ought to / ought develop a good relationship with the puppy.

6. You are supposed to make / making sure that the puppy understands your signals.

7. The puppy also must does / do what you want, too.

8. Dogs aren't able / aren't able to concentrate for as long as you.

9. A young dog may to learn / learn a few simple tricks within a week.

10. The dog have to / has to enjoy the lessons.

11. Soon the dog will know / knowing your commands.

12. Some dogs be able to / are able to learn faster than others, of course.

13. Don't punish your dog if it can't / can to learn quickly.

14. You maybe / might come to the conclusion that your dog just isn't a performer.

15. Both you and your pet will to / will be happier if the dog receives a lot of praise.

16. The dog is allowed to do / is allowed to did tricks for fun.

PRACTICE **39** Statements and Questions with Modals

WH-WORD	MODAL (+ N'T)	SUBJECT	MODAL (+ N'T)	VERB (BASE FORM)	COMPLEMENT	SHORT ANSWER
		He	**can**	have	a cat in his apartment.	
		He	**can't**	have	a dog.	
	Can	he		have	a bird?	No, he **can't.**
What	**can**	he		have	in his apartment?	
Why	**can't**	he		have	a dog?	
		Who	**can**	own	animals in an apartment?	

EXERCISE 1 Make a question with the modal or expression and subject in parentheses.

Example: **Q:** (can / who) _____ *Who can* _____ show us the way to the theater?

A: Harry can.

1. **Q:** (we /should) _____ leave the baby here when we shop?
   A: No, we mustn't do that.

2. **Q:** (why / we / not / could) _____ fix this broken printer?
   A: It is too complicated. We need an expert.

3. **Q:** (they / be permitted to / where) _____ sunbathe?
   A: Only at the pool or the beach.

4. **Q:** (must / I / where) _____ pay this overdue book fine?
   A: At the library.

5. **Q:** (people / how many / may) _____ be in this car at one time?
   A: No more than five.

6. **Q:** (will / not / it) _____ rain tonight?
   A: I don't think so. The clouds are clearing.

7. **Q:** (has to / who) _____ clean the house today?
   A: We do, unfortunately.

8. **Q:** (be able to / you) _____ swim the length of the pool five times?
   A: Not me. Ask someone else.

9. **Q:** (might / when / you) _____ come over?
   A: Just as soon as I finish what I'm doing.

10. **Q:** (be supposed to / who) _____ give him the bad news?
    A: I think you ought to.

EXERCISE 2 Unscramble the words to make a question with a modal expression.

Example: the homework / hand in / tomorrow / I / may

May I hand in the homework tomorrow ?

1. the hospital / permitted / when / you / to leave / are

_____?

2. I / this purchase / a credit card / pay for / with / can

_____?

3. ought to / for / who / pay / the restaurant dinner

_____?

4. without / to travel / people / why / allowed / a passport / aren't

_____?

5. should / to / give / we / our papers / who

_____?

6. able / graduate / when / she / to / will / be

_____?

7. a car / must / in your country / drive / how old / you / to / be

_____?

8. we / are / the video / allowed / how long / keep / to

_____?

PRACTICE 40 — *Must, Have To, Have Got To, and Be Supposed To*

FORMAL OR OFFICIAL	INFORMAL	EXPLANATION
Everyone **must** obey the law.	Everyone **has to** obey the law. Everyone **has got to** obey the law. Everyone **is supposed to** obey the law.	Legal obligation
We **must** operate on this patient immediately.	We **have to** operate on this patient immediately. We**'ve got to** operate on this patient immediately.	Urgency
I **have to** wash my car.	I**'ve got to** wash my car.	Personal necessity

LANGUAGE NOTES:
1. We don't usually use *have got to* for questions and negatives.
2. *Must* has no past form. The past of both *must* and *have to* is *had to*.

EXERCISE 1 Fill in the blank with *must* for rules and laws. Fill in the blank with *have / has to* or *have / has got to* for personal necessities and urgent situations.

Example: Taxpayers _____*must*_____ mail their tax forms before midnight on April 15.

1. I _____ pick up milk on my way home.

2. Taxi drivers _____ display their ID cards.

3. Nonmembers _____ pay at the reception desk.

4. I'm so tired. I _____ start going to bed earlier.

5. You kids _____ wash up before dinner.

6. Students _____ pay their fees by the last day of January.

7. We _____ get to the bank before it closes.

8. Swimmers _____ not bring glass bottles into the pool area.

9. Employees _____ wash their hands before returning to work.

10. I _____ find a part-time job to cover my expenses.

11. Pedestrians _____ cross the street at the crosswalk.

12. I _____ give you back your book.

13. Students _____ not eat in the library.

14. We _____ buy a new car. This one breaks down.

15. We _____ pay her back.

16. You _____ show your passport before boarding the plane.
17. I _____ buy my mother a birthday present.
18. I _____ get my wife to the hospital before this baby is born.

EXERCISE 2 Fill in each blank with an appropriate verb.

Example: Parents have to *protect their children.* _____

1. The president must _____
2. In the summer students don't have to _____
3. Every car owner has to _____
4. Professional drivers must _____
5. A good teacher is supposed to _____
6. Every landlord has got to _____
7. People who live in a dormitory must not _____
8. People who live in a dormitory don't have to _____
9. Police officers mustn't _____
10. Retired people don't have to _____
11. Athletes in training are supposed to _____
12. Trainers of athletes have got to _____

EXERCISE 3 Finish these sentences telling what you and other people *must, have to, have got to,* and *are supposed to* do in life.

Example: I have to *study every night.* _____

1. People have to _____
2. I have got to _____
3. I must _____
4. Children must _____
5. They are supposed to _____
6. I am supposed to _____

PRACTICE 41 Can, Could, May, Be Able To, Be Permitted To, and Be Allowed To

MODAL	ALTERNATE EXPRESSION	EXPLANATION
She **can** pay up to $300 for her plane ticket.	**It is possible** for her to pay up to $300 for her plane ticket.	Possibility
I **can't** get the door to open. I **can** speak three languages.	We **are not able to** get the door to open.	Ability
We **can't** take more than two bags onto the plane.	We **are not allowed to / are not permitted to** take more than two bags onto the plane.	Permission
You **may** leave whenever you want to.	You **are allowed to / are permitted** to leave whenever you want to.	Permission
I **couldn't** operate a computer three years ago, but I **can** now.	I **wasn't able to** operate a computer three years ago, but I **am able to** now.	Past ability
I **couldn't** drive until I got a license, but now I **can.**	I **wasn't permitted to** drive until I got a license, but now I **am permitted to / am allowed to.**	Past permission

EXERCISE 1 Underline each modal expression and change it to the negative past tense.

Example: He <u>can</u> pay the credit card bill today.

(last week) *He couldn't pay the credit card bill last week.*

1. Amy can play the flute very well this year.

   (last year) _____

2. Janet is allowed to take out books from the library this week.

   (last week) _____

3. We are able to play soccer as a team this month.

   (two months ago) _____

4. It is possible for Eric to earn a lot of money in this job.

   (in his previous job) _____

5. Lily can pronounce English very well this semester.

   (last semester) _____

6. They may live in the dormitories this term.

   (last term) _____

EXERCISE 2 Underline the modal or modal expression and write an alternative expression in its place.

Example: I <u>can't</u> pay $1,200 a year for car insurance.

It isn't possible for me to pay $1,200 a year for car insurance.

1. My sister can babysit on Saturday nights.

   _____

2. Don can play the guitar and the piano.

   _____

3. Nancy can use Ed's van this weekend.

   _____

4. The children may watch TV until 9:00 p.m.

   _____

5. I could sing very well when I was young, but now I can't.

   _____

6. We could drive without seatbelts two years ago, but now we can't.

   _____

7. It isn't possible for me to take a vacation soon.

   _____

8. The little boy wasn't allowed to stay up late, but now he is.

   _____

9. The runner wasn't able to cut time off his speed this year.

   _____

10. She isn't able to pay her rent on time every month.

    _____

11. He isn't permitted to plan the parade.

    _____

12. The students are allowed to take the test home.

    _____

PRACTICE 42 *Should* and *Had Better*

EXAMPLE	EXPLANATION
You **should** talk to a counselor about the problem with your math class. You **shouldn't** get so upset.	For advice, use *should:* *Should* = It's a good idea (thing). *Shouldn't* = It's a bad idea (thing).
You **had better** renew your visa before you leave the country. You **had better not** forget to do it, or you won't be able to get back in.	For a warning, use *had better (not):* Something bad can happen if you don't follow this advice.

LANGUAGE NOTES:

The contraction for *had* (in *had better*) is *'d:*

I'd   you'd   he'd   she'd   we'd   they'd

EXERCISE 1 Label the following sentences: *This is good advice* or *This is a warning.*

Examples: We should ask the doctor about vitamins.   *This is good advice.*

You'd better not be impolite to your boss.   *This is a warning.*

1. You should see the dentist about your bad tooth.

2. We had better not eat any more French fries or potato chips.

3. He should pick up some milk and bread on the way home tonight.

4. They'd better keep their passports in a safe place.

5. We should wash the dishes before we watch TV tonight.

6. Parents should teach their children to be honest.

7. She'd better study harder or she will fail the test.

8. We'd better not forget our keys in the car again.

EXERCISE 2 Rewrite each affirmative sentence as a negative sentence. Rewrite each negative sentence as an affirmative sentence.

Example: You had better not drive slowly.   *You'd better drive slowly.*

1. You'd better stay up all night before the test.

   _____

2. She should arrive late to work every day.

   _____

3. We'd better not do our laundry this week.

   _____

4. I had better gain more weight.

   _____

5. They shouldn't be kind to their students.

   _____

6. You had better forget to pack your bags for tomorrow.

   _____

EXERCISE 3 Your friend is going to a different country. Choose eight expressions from the box. Then use *should* (for good or bad ideas) or *had better* (for legal necessities or warnings) to give advice. You can make some of the sentences negative.

Example: *You had better make a doctor's appointment.* _____

apply for a passport	~~make a doctor's appointment~~	take an umbrella
obtain a visa	study the language	lose your airplane tickets
pack your swimsuit	take a bilingual dictionary	change some money
take some medicine for an upset stomach		take some gifts for people there
give your family an emergency telephone number		

Where is your friend going to go? _____

1. _____
2. _____
3. _____
4. _____
5. _____
6. _____
7. _____
8. _____

PRACTICE 43 Negatives of Modals and Related Expressions

EXAMPLE	EXPLANATION
Passengers **must not** remove their seatbelts at this time.	Use *must not* for prohibition. These things are against the law or rules.
You **cannot** have a dog in my apartment. You **may not** use a calculator on the mathematics exam.	Use *cannot* or *may not* to show no permission. The meaning is about the same as *must not*.
You**'re not supposed to** park here longer than 15 minutes.	Use *be not supposed to* for prohibition. These things are against the law or rules.
You **are not supposed to** drive quickly near schools or in the city.	When reporting a rule, people use *be not supposed to* more than *must not*. Remember, *must not* has an official tone.
She **doesn't have to** take the entrance examination because she doesn't want to go to a university.	A person can perform a particular action if he or she wants to, but he or she has no obligation to do this thing.
You **shouldn't** watch so much TV.	*Shouldn't* is for advice, not rules.
You**'d better not** miss the final exam, or you'll fail the course.	*Had better not* is for a warning.

LANGUAGE NOTE:

Ought to is used in affirmative statements. Avoid the use of this expression in negative statements or questions.

EXERCISE 1 Circle the better negative modal to complete the sentence.

Example: They are not supposed to /(must not) break the law.

1. On Sundays I <u>don't have to / must not</u> get up early.

2. He <u>doesn't have to / cannot</u> be late to work again, or else he'll lose his job.

3. Everyone enjoys the wildflowers, but people <u>shouldn't / don't have to</u> pick them.

4. We <u>had better not / cannot</u> make too much noise or we'll wake the baby.

5. You <u>may not / shouldn't</u> lose control of your credit card spending.

6. At a birthday party, you <u>must not / shouldn't</u> refuse birthday cake.

7. In most cultures, children <u>cannot / are not supposed to</u> correct their parents.

8. No, you <u>may not / shouldn't</u> stay up all night long because you're seven years old and you have school tomorrow.

9. She <u>is not supposed to / must not</u> ignore her parking ticket.

10. In some cultures, people <u>don't have to / cannot</u> visit other people without a gift.

EXERCISE 2 Decide if the statement means *a prohibition, no permission, no obligation, advice,* or *a warning.* Write the correct explanation next to each sentence.

Example: _____*a warning*_____ You had better not eat that fruit. You are allergic to it.

1. _____ You are not supposed to drive when you are very tired.
2. _____ People cannot take books from the library without a library card.
3. _____ He must not tell lies about other people.
4. _____ You had better not call in sick to work.
5. _____ We must not forget our father's birthday this year.
6. _____ They are not supposed to make noise in the dormitory.
7. _____ You may not gossip about my friends.
8. _____ I don't have to return the money you gave me. You said it was a gift.
9. _____ We shouldn't take off our coats in this cold weather.
10. _____You are not supposed to enter the office during a meeting.

EXERCISE 3 Finish each sentence with your own ideas.

Example: Children aren't supposed to _____*watch violent movies.*_____

1. Children should not _____
2. Babies can't _____
3. Parents don't have to _____
4. Teachers must not _____
5. Secondary school students aren't allowed to _____
6. Tourists should not _____
7. Teenagers had better not _____
8. If you have a computer, you don't have to _____
9. Employees must not _____
10. Dogs are not supposed to _____

PRACTICE 44 *Will, May,* and Might

EXAMPLE	EXPLANATION
My lease **will** expire on April 30.	Certainty about the future
My landlord **might** raise my rent at that time. I **may** move.	Possibility or uncertainty about the future
The teacher isn't here today. She **may** be sick. **or** She **might** be sick.	Possibility or uncertainty about the present

EXERCISE 1

Circle the better modal to show that this sentence is about certainty (*will*) or uncertainty / possibility (*may / might*).

Example: My friends might / (will) come to dinner Friday at 6:30 p.m.

1. You might / will get a wonderful job when you graduate from college.
2. The world will / may become peaceful for the next one hundred years.
3. All the students may / will get excellent grades on the final exam.
4. She may / will have a hair salon appointment at 5:00 p.m.
5. We may / will have a little rain tonight. The forecast wasn't clear.
6. I don't really know. They might / move to Venezuela next year.
7. I will / may come to see you tomorrow morning at 9:30 a.m.
8. Your car sounds a little strange. You might / will have to go to the mechanic.
9. My first paycheck might / will arrive tomorrow.
10. George and Debbie will / may marry on June 21.

EXERCISE 2

Does the sentence explain a possibility about *the present* or a possibility about *the future?*

Example: My cat isn't in the house. He may be hiding. ___present___

1. Their television isn't on. Her husband may be reading. ______________________
2. The newspaper said we may have warm weather tomorrow. ______________________
3. You may have a fever. Your forehead feels hot. ______________________
4. You may get a cold. Many people were sick at school. ______________________
5. I may pay someone to tutor me in college math. ______________________
6. She may go on a world tour someday. ______________________

EXERCISE 3 Make five sentences about what you *will* definitely do in the coming year, and then make five more about what you *may / might* do.

Example: *I will learn to paint my house.* ____   *I may learn to grow vegetables.* ____

will

1. _____
2. _____
3. _____
4. _____
5. _____

may or *might*

1. _____
2. _____
3. _____
4. _____
5. _____

EXERCISE 4 Make five sentences about things that you definitely *won't do* in the future. Then make five more about things that you *may not / might not* do.

Example: *I won't buy a parrot.* ____   *I may not find a nice, cheap apartment.* ____

won't

1. _____
2. _____
3. _____
4. _____
5. _____

may not or *might not*

1. _____
2. _____
3. _____
4. _____
5. _____

PRACTICE 45 Using Modals for Politeness

TO ASK PERMISSION	EXPLANATION
May **Can** } I write you a check? **Could**	*May* and *could* are considered more polite than *can* by some speakers of English.

TO REQUEST THAT ANOTHER PERSON DO SOMETHING	EXPLANATION
Can **Could** } you plug it in? **Will** **Would**	For a request, *could* and *would* are softer than *can* and *will*.

TO EXPRESS A WANT OR DESIRE	EXPLANATION
Would you **like** to try out the computer? Yes, I **would like** to see if it works. I**'d like** a glass of water.	*Would like* has the same meaning as *want*. *Would like* is softer than *want*. The contraction for *would* after a pronoun is *'d*.

TO EXPRESS A PREFERENCE	EXPLANATION
Would you **rather** pay with cash or by credit card? I**'d rather** pay by credit card (than with cash).	We use *or* in questions with *would rather*. We use *than* in statements.

EXERCISE 1 Choose the more polite modal and add it to the statement or question.

Example: (may / can) _____ May _____ I leave now?

1. (want / would like)   I _____ a cup of hot chocolate, please.

2. (can / could) Professor, _____ I visit you during office hours today?

3. (will / would) _____ you kids clean the kitchen after dinner?

4. (will / could) _____ you hand me that dictionary, please?

5. (can / may) *Child:* _____ we read some of your comics?

6. (would like / want) *Friend:* I _____ to play ball first.

7. (want / would like)   I _____ to see a menu, please.

8. (could / will) _____ you get me a drink of water while you're up?

9. (can / may) _____ you look for a larger size shirt, please?

10. (may / can) Grandfather, _____ I borrow your car tonight?

11. (would / could) _____ I borrow your pen?

12. (would / may) _____ you help me carry the desk?

EXERCISE 2 Read the description of the speakers and the situation. Then write an appropriate polite request (question) or sentence.

Example: A professor asks a student to stop by her office today.

Would you stop by my office today, please?

1. A sister asks a brother to take any telephone messages for her.

   _____

2. A policewoman asks a driver to show her his driver's license.

   _____

3. One student offers to show another student around the college campus.

   _____

4. A student asks a monitor in the computer lab for help.

   _____

5. A supervisor offers the employee the choice of more money or more vacation time.

   _____

6. A waitperson offers to show a customer the dessert menu.

   _____

EXERCISE 3 Change each of the following sentences to make it more polite.

Example: Open the door.

Could you please open the door for me?

1. I want to borrow your skates.

   _____

2. Give me the rice.

   _____

3. I want change for a dollar.

   _____

Overview of the Present Perfect Tense

SUBJECT	HAVE / HAS	PAST PARTICIPLE	COMPLEMENT
The world map	has	changed	a great deal in the past 40 years.
Some countries	have	chosen	new names for themselves.
Others	have	become	independent.
She	has	been	happy to study geography.

REGULAR VERBS

Base Form	Past Form	Past Participle
study	studied	studied
look	looked	looked

IRREGULAR VERBS

leave	left	left
understand	understood	understood
come	came	come
run	ran	run
draw	drew	drawn
fly	flew	flown
know	knew	known
wear	wore	worn
break	broke	broken
choose	chose	chosen
speak	spoke	spoken
steal	stole	stolen
begin	began	begun
drink	drank	drunk
ring	rang	rung
swim	swam	swum
rise	rose	risen
bite	bit	bitten
drive	drove	driven
ride	rode	ridden
write	wrote	written
be	was/were	been
eat	ate	eaten
fall	fell	fallen
give	gave	given
see	saw	seen
make	made	made
take	took	taken
do	did	done
forget	forgot	forgotten
have / has	had	had
lie	lay	lain

EXERCISE 1 Complete each sentence with *have* or *has*.

Example: I _____*have*_____ chosen to tell you about my father.

1. My father's life _____ been very different from his father's life.
2. He _____ worked as a veterinarian for 20 years.
3. He and my mother _____ made a good home for me.
4. He _____ cured hundreds of sick dogs, cats, and farm animals.
5. I _____ learned quite a bit about animals from him.
6. My sister and I _____ helped him during school vacations.
7. We _____ gone with him to animal emergencies.
8. He _____ taken me to watch him work many times.
9. Farmers _____ come to him for help with their cows and horses.
10. Now you _____ heard a little about my father's life. I am very proud of him.

EXERCISE 2 Complete each sentence with *have* or *has* plus the correct past participle of the verb in parentheses.

Example: I (travel / not) _____*have not traveled*_____ to many cities in my life.

She (eat) _____*has eaten*_____ in expensive restaurants a few times.

1. I (know / not) _____ many interesting people.
2. My friends and I (enjoy) _____ other cities.
3. You (begin) _____ to travel a lot in the past year.
4. You and I (write) _____ many postcards to our friends.
5. My professor (take) _____ time to do more research.
6. He (speak) _____ to us about his interest in languages.
7. My doctor (give) _____ me a prescription for my cold.
8. It (be) _____ very difficult to get a doctor's appointment.
9. They (start / not) _____ to jog for their health.
10. The joggers (run) _____ 10 miles so far this week.
11. That dog (bite) _____ two people up until now.
12. She (wear) _____ that blue dress only once.
13. They (not / see) _____ that movie yet.
14. The movers (drive) _____ to the wrong address.

PRACTICE 47 Statements and Questions with the Present Perfect Tense

WH–WORD	HAVE / HAS HAVEN'T / HASN'T	SUBJECT	HAVE / HAS HAVEN'T / HASN'T	PAST PARTICIPLE	COMPLEMENT	SHORT ANSWER
		I	have	been	busy.	
		I	haven't	been	available	
	Have	you		been	tired?	Yes, I have.
Why	have	you		been	busy?	
Why	haven't	you		been	available?	
		Who	has	been	busy?	

EXERCISE 1 Answer each of the following questions using the present perfect tense to complete each sentence.

Example: **Q:** How long have you lived in this city?

A: *I've lived here for only a few months.*

1. **Q:** Have you ever been to Moscow?

   A: _____

2. **Q:** How much money have you spent on books this month?

   A: _____

3. **Q:** Have you ever been on TV?

   A: _____

4. **Q:** How many movies have you seen this month?

   A: _____

5. **Q:** Has it rained here recently?

   A: _____

6. **Q:** How long have you studied English grammar?

   A: _____

7. **Q:** Have you decided what to do after you finish studying English?

   A: _____

8. **Q:** What is something that you've always dreamed of doing?

   A: _____

9. **Q:** Have you ever gone to a movie by yourself?

   A: _____

10. **Q:** How many times have you moved from one home to another?

    A: _____

Create present perfect questions based on the words in parentheses. Answer each question about yourself.

Example:

    Q: (how many times / have / bad dreams) *How many times have you had bad dreams?*

    A: *I've had bad dreams many times.*

1. (have / ever / speak / in front of one hundred people)

    Q: _____

    A: _____

2. (how long / have / lived in this city)

    Q: _____

    A: _____

3. (how many times / have / a good job)

    Q: _____

    A: _____

4. (why / have / not / jump / out of a plane)

    Q: _____

    A: _____

5. (where / have / live / in your life)

    Q: _____

    A: _____

6. (when / have / study / recently)

    Q: _____

    A: _____

7. (what / have / done / for fun / this week)

    Q: _____

    A: _____

8. (have / ever / make / a difficult decision)

    Q: _____

    A: _____

48 Continuation from Past to Present Tense

EXAMPLE	EXPLANATION
We **have lived** in this house for 10 years.	Use *for* + an amount of time: *for two years, for ten months, for a long time,* etc.
She **has been** out of town **since** Monday.	Use *since* + date, month, year, etc. to show when the action began: *since April, since 1998, since May 2, since Tuesday,* etc.
She **has been** worried about him **since** she got his message.	Use *since* + a clause to show the start of a continuous action. The verb in the *since* clause is in the simple past tense: *since she got his message.*
How long has your brother **lived** with you?	Use *how long* to ask about the amount of time from the past to the present.
I **have always loved** to cook.	Use the present perfect tense with *always* to show that an action began in the past and continues to the present.
I **have never gone** to Spain.	Use the present perfect tense with *never* to show that something has not occurred from the past to the present.

LANGUAGE NOTE:

We use the present perfect tense to show that an action or state started in the past and continues to the present.

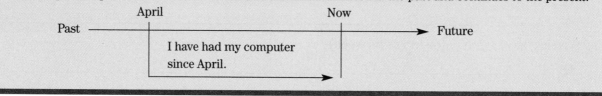

Past ————— April ————————— Now ————————→ Future

I have had my computer since April.

EXERCISE 1 Read the following two paragraphs. Underline all of the present perfect verbs. There are 15 present perfect verbs to find.

What a flood!   (**Example**)   It <u>has rained</u> for five days now. The water has risen gradually until it has covered the streets and the sidewalks. The lower parts of the town have sunk below the water. Most people who live near the river have left the town. It has rained here before, but I have never seen rain like this.

The flood has been a disaster for the town. Everyone who has purchased a boat has been asked to bring the boats to rescue people and animals. We have always swum in the water before, but now it's dirty and polluted. My family has left the town. We have lived in a shelter since April 14. Some families have been here for three weeks. I have heard of floods like this, but I have never known one.

EXERCISE 2 Add a time expression to each sentence.

Example: (never) I have met her.

I have never met her.

1. (for five days)   She has studied for the test.

   _____

2. (always)   He has lived here.

   _____

3. (since you got a job)   I haven't seen you.

   _____

4. (never) We have visited the art museum.

   _____

5. (since Tuesday)   They have waited for the letter.

   _____

6. (since December)   You have had that coat.

   _____

7. (for a long time)   The clock hasn't rung.

   _____

8. (since he ate some fish)   He has felt sick.

   _____

9. (since I borrowed the money)   I have avoided you.

   _____

10. (for one month)   We haven't received a call from her.

    _____

EXERCISE 3 Complete each of the following sentences about yourself, your family, or your friends with the present perfect verb tense and the time expression in parentheses.

Example: (for six months)   _My sister hasn't seen my parents for six months._

1. (since I began school)   _____

2. (for one week)   _____

3. (always)   _____

4. (since 1999)   _____

5. (for a long time)   _____

PRACTICE 49 — The Simple Present versus the Present Perfect Tenses

SIMPLE PRESENT TENSE	PRESENT PERFECT TENSE
I **am** in the United States now.	I **have been** in the United States for 2 years.
She **has** a car.	She **has had** her car since March.
I **love** my job.	I **have** always **loved** my job.
She **doesn't have** a job.	She **has** never **had** a full-time job.

LANGUAGE NOTE:
The simple present tense refers only to the present time. The present perfect tense with *for, since, always,* or *never* connects the past to the present time.

EXERCISE 1 Read each present tense sentence. Then use *for, since, always, or never* with the information in the parentheses to write a present perfect sentence that connects the past to the present time.

Example: I know Maria. (five years)

I have known her for five years.

1. She owns a house. (last summer)

2. Eduardo lives in this city. (a year and a half)

3. The twins are in the hospital. (They were born two days ago.)

4. My aunt is an excellent cook. (always)

5. Sarah doesn't have a car. (never)

6. Gina and Tom are married. (five years)

7. Marco belongs to the volleyball club. (April)

8. He doesn't belong to the soccer club. (never)

9. Allison doesn't live with her family now. (the beginning of the year)

10. She eats all her meals in the university cafeteria.   (last spring)

_____

11. Andy and his roommate live in an apartment near campus.   (six months)

_____

12. I am a sales clerk in this department store.   (three years)

_____

13. Fran is a student at the English Language Institute.   (January)

_____

14. Gina is absent from class again today.   (Monday)

_____

15. He is on a diet.   (a few months)

_____

16. She wears the ring he gave her.   (they got married in 1972)

_____

17. My father speaks Spanish.   (always)

_____

EXERCISE 2 Read each present perfect answer provided. Then write an appropriate simple present tense question.

Example: **Q:** _Do you own this house?_____

A: Yes, I've owned it since 1998.

1. **Q:** _____
   A: Yes, he has belonged to that health club for about a year now.

2. **Q:** _____
   A: No, I've never enjoyed exercise.

3. **Q:** _____
   A: I've tried to, but I've never been successful.

4. **Q:** _____
   A: No. Actually, she's never come to see us.

5. **Q:** _____
   A: Yes. We've gone to see her several times.

WH– WORD	HAVE / HAS HAVEN'T / HASN'T	SUBJECT	HAVE / HAS HAVEN'T / HASN'T	BEEN	VERB + –ING	COMPLEMENT	SHORT ANSWER
		Carol	has	been	living	in the United States	
		She	hasn't	been	living	in Italy.	
	Has	she		been	living	in New York?	No, she hasn't.
How long	has	she		been	living	in the United States?	
Why	hasn't	she		been	living	in Italy?	
		Who	has	been	living	in Italy?	

LANGUAGE NOTES:

1. With some verbs (such as *live, work, study, teach, wear*), we can use either the present perfect or the present perfect continuous tense with actions that began in the past and continue to the present. There is very little difference in meaning.
2. If the action is still happening right now, at this minute, it is better to use the present perfect continuous tense.
3. Remember that we do not use the continuous form with nonaction verbs. Some nonaction verbs are: *like, love, have, want, need, know, remember, hear, own, see, seem, understand.*

EXERCISE 1 Choose the better verb tense for each set of underlined verbs.

Example: Mother (has seemed) / has been seeming upset since the accident on Monday.

1. How long have you watched / have you been watching this movie?
2. I have lived / have been living in this city for five years.
3. I have liked / been liking this city since I moved here.
4. My daughter has always loved / has always been loving to eat vegetables.
5. Why has she studied / has been studying English since September?
6. How long have you owned / have you been owning this car?
7. He has worked / has been working as an engineer for many years.
8. How much of what she's saying have you understood / have you been understanding?
9. We have eaten / have been eating dinner since the roast came out of the oven.
10. What have you been doing / have you done these days?

EXERCISE 2 Fill in each blank with the present perfect continuous tense of the verbs in the box. Choose an appropriate verb from the box.

wait	watch	live	practice	look	date	tell	write
save	cook	exercise	expect	stay	play	read	

Examples: Now that we _____*have been dating*_____ for a year, I think we should get married.

    or How long _____*have*_____ you _____*been dating*_____ Joe?

1. The soup _____ for two hours. I think it's ready.

2. I _____ for so long that my hand hurts.

3. How long _____ she _____? If he doesn't arrive soon, she'll give up.

4. He _____ everywhere for his keys, and he can't find them.

5. The band _____ for such a long time that I think the concert must be almost over.

6. Why _____ I _____ for two hours? My muscles are going to be really sore tomorrow.

7. You _____ TV all evening. You have to stop now and do your homework.

8. Renée _____ in Montreal, but she's moving to Toronto next month.

9. Come in. We _____ you.

10. I _____ this book for hours. My eyes are starting to get tired.

11. Who _____ me about your train trip across northern Mexico recently?

12. The children _____ up late every night this summer, but next week when school starts, they have to go to bed early again.

13. _____ you _____ the piano lately?

14. She _____ her money, and now she's ready to buy a new computer.

PRACTICE 51 The Present Perfect Tense with Indefinite Time in the Past

EXAMPLE	EXPLANATION
Have you ever **used** the Internet? Yes, I **have.** **Have** you ever **gone** to a family reunion? Yes, I've **gone** to many family reunions. **Has** Carol **ever gone** to Italy? No, she **never has.**	A question with *ever* asks about any time between the past and the present. Put *ever* between the subject and the main verb. We can answer an *ever* question with a frequency response: *a few times, many times, often, never.*
Has Carol **met** her cousin **yet?** Yes, she **has already met** her cousin. **Have** you **cleaned** your room **yet?** No, I **haven't cleaned** it **yet.** or No, not **yet.**	*Yet* and *already* refer to an indefinite time in the near past. Use *yet* in questions and negatives. Use *already* in affirmative statements.
Have you **washed** the dishes yet? Yes. I **have just washed** them.	*Just* shows that something happened very recently.

LANGUAGE NOTE:

We use the present perfect tense to refer to an action that occurred at an indefinite time in the past and still has importance to the present situation:

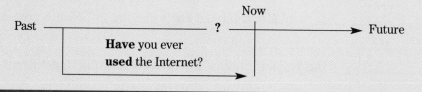

EXERCISE 1 Fill in each blank with *ever, already, yet,* or *just.* In some cases more than one of the words can be used.

Example: Haven't you finished _____ *yet?* _____

1. You're too late; the doctor has _____ left for the day.

2. Have you _____ ridden a horse? It's fun!

3. I've _____ invited him to the party.

4. I'm so tired of that book! I've _____ read it three times.

5. Why haven't you written him _____?

6. Haven't you _____ been lonely?

7. Don't sit in that chair! I've _____ painted it.

8. I've _____ seen Hernando, and he looks upset.

9. She hasn't contacted us _____, but I'm sure she will soon.

10. We've _____ saved all of the money that our children will need for their university education.

11. I haven't told her about my plans _____ .

12. Have you _____ read an entire novel in English?

13. We have to wait here because their plane hasn't arrived _____ .

14. You can't take any more time off because you've _____ used up all of your vacation and sick days for this year.

EXERCISE 2 Unscramble the words to write correct statements and questions.

Example: found / new / I / already / roommate / a / have

I have already found a new roommate. _____

1. the door / my roommate / just / in / come / has

_____ .

2. ever / the oil / this car / checked / haven't / you / in

_____ ?

3. she / to / already / three universities / applied / has

_____ .

4. haven't / my request / replied / yet / they / to

_____ .

5. this meat / anyone / the refrigerator / why / in / put / hasn't / yet

_____ ?

6. just / their landlord / has / them / to move / asked

_____ .

7. had / bad news / you / anyone / have / to / ever / to break

_____ ?

8. the checkbook / balanced / yet / haven't / I

_____ .

9. ever / why / him / told / you / haven't / how / feel / really / you

_____ ?

10. seen / have / we / movie / already / that / romantic

_____ .

PRACTICE 52 Overview of Gerunds

EXAMPLES	USE OF GERUND
Camping is a popular outdoor activity.	As a subject A gerund takes a singular verb.
Many people **enjoy swimming**. I **miss seeing** you in my class. They **avoid studying** on Saturday nights.	As an object Some verbs are followed by a gerund: *enjoy, miss, avoid, quit, suggest*.
Some people are in favor **of hunting,** while others are opposed to it. I'm **interested in learning** more about computers.	As an object of a preposition Some adjectives are followed by a preposition.
Today you can buy your clothes **by shopping** on the Internet. I thought **about going** to a job counselor. You should practice **by studying** interview questions.	In an adverbial phrase Some verbs are followed by a preposition.
I like to **go shopping**.	In special expressions with go *Go* + a gerund is used in many idiomatic expressions: *go jogging, go dancing, go swimming, go fishing, go shopping*.

LANGUAGE NOTES:

1. A gerund phrase is a gerund + a noun: *finding a job, learning English*.
2. We can put *not* in front of a gerund (phrase) to make it negative:
     Not having a job is frustrating.
3. These verbs can be followed by a gerund:

admit	discuss	mind	put off
appreciate	dislike	miss	quit
avoid	enjoy	permit	recommend
can't help	finish	postpone	risk
consider	keep	practice	suggest

EXERCISE 1 Fill in each blank with the gerund form of one of the verbs in the box.

	climb	wash	fish	camp
~~smoke~~	practice	study	do	diet	clean
sail	think	help	exercise	play

Example: _____Smoking_____ is not allowed on many airplane flights these days.

1. First we dug up some worms, and then we went _____.
2. _____ basketball is a good way to relax.
3. _____ all night before a test can make you tired and tense.
4. I bought a special rope for mountain _____.
5. There's a good breeze today. Let's go _____.
6. I am trying to lose weight by _____ and _____ regularly.
7. I know you want to avoid _____ the dishes.
8. Even during an exam she can't help _____ about her grades.
9. _____ my apartment is not my favorite activity.
10. He improved his performance by _____ over and over.
11. You shouldn't delay _____ the things that need to be done.
12. _____ patients to get well is a nurse's job.

EXERCISE 2 Answer each question with a sentence that contains a gerund.

Example: **Q:** What's an activity that makes you tired?

A: _____Studying grammar_____ makes me tired.

1. **Q:** When do you grocery shop?
   A: I go _____
2. **Q:** What's something that you really enjoy doing?
   A: I really enjoy _____
3. **Q:** What's something that you need to practice more often?
   A: I need to practice _____
4. **Q:** What's a suggestion that you made to someone recently?
   A: I recommended _____
5. **Q:** How do you quit that bad habit?
   A: I quit by _____
6. **Q:** What's something that you don't like doing?
   A: I dislike _____
7. **Q:** What activity bores you?
   A: I consider _____
8. **Q:** What's something you often put off doing?
   A: I put off _____

PRACTICE 53 Overview of Infinitives

EXAMPLE	EXPLANATION
I want **to find** a job.	An infinitive is used after certain verbs.
I want you **to help** me.	An object can be added before an infinitive.
I'm happy **to help** you.	An infinitive can follow certain adjectives.
It's important **to write** a good résumé.	An infinitive follows certain expressions with *it*.
He went to a counselor **to get** advice.	An infinitive is used to show purpose.

EXERCISE 1 Fill in each blank with the infinitive form of a verb from the box.

pay	understand	give	operate	tell	earn
travel	stay	swim	win	call	speak
	drive	eat	communicate		

Example: It's going to take more money than this_____*to pay*_____ for your purchases.

1. My parents didn't want me _____ to another country alone.

2. Children, wait a minute. This soup is too hot _____.

3. In some countries it's illegal _____ a car without insurance.

4. Many people today use e-mail _____ with each other.

5. Her parents made her promise not _____ out late.

6. They forgot _____ us what time they'd be arriving.

7. It can be dangerous _____ in the ocean.

8. His pronunciation is a little bit hard _____.

9. Many parents tell their children not _____ to strangers.

10. Patients can just push this button _____ a nurse.

11. Cars with big engines are more expensive _____.

12. Some people come from wealthy families, but most people have _____ their own money.

13. The robbers forced the man _____ them all his money.

14. You were really lucky _____ that contest.

EXERCISE 2 Unscramble the words to write correct statements and questions.

Example: my vocabulary words / to write / like / in a notebook / I

I like to write my vocabulary words in a notebook.

1. to write / my compositions / my computer / use / I

_____

2. easy / the application forms / it / to complete / wasn't

_____

3. me / a souvenir / my brother / to bring / wants / him

_____

4. is / handwriting / to read / your / hard

_____

5. expect / my money / my parents / carefully / me / to spend

_____

6. is / to make / easy / popcorn / and / quick

_____

7. to study / it / for you / convenient / in the library / is

_____?

EXERCISE 3 Answer each question with a complete sentence that contains an infinitive.

Example: What's something that takes a long time to learn?

It takes a long time to learn to cook well.

1. What's something important that a family member has asked you to do?
   A: _____

2. What are three things that people use to write with?
   A: _____

3. What's something that children are too young to do safely?
   A: _____

4. What's something that is important to do every day?
   A: _____

5. What's something that you need to do today?
   A: _____

PRACTICE 54 Infinitives as Subjects

EXAMPLE	EXPLANATION
It takes a long time to **learn** a foreign language really well. **It**'s fun **to practice** with my classmates.	An infinitive can be used as the subject of a sentence. We can begin the sentence with *it* and delay the infinitive.
It isn't hard **for children** to learn a foreign language. **It**'s more difficult **for adults** to learn one.	Include *for* + noun or object pronoun to make a statement that is true for a specific person or group.

LANGUAGE NOTES:

1. When we use an infinitive after these adjectives, the first word in the sentence is most likely to be *it*:

dangerous	good	necessary
difficult	great	possible
easy	hard	sad
expensive	important	wrong
fun	impossible	

2. There is no difference in meaning between an infinitive subject and a gerund subject:

   It's important *to arrive on time.*   *Arriving on time* is important.

EXERCISE 1 Complete each sentence with an infinitive phrase. You can add an object if you like.

Example: It isn't healthy _(for me) to eat a lot of greasy foods._ _____

1. It is impossible _____

2. It's frightening _____

3. It's so much fun _____

4. It's very relaxing _____

5. It's sad _____

6. It's wrong _____

7. It's important _____

8. It is boring _____

9. It's foolish _____

10. It's illegal _____

EXERCISE 2 Rewrite each sentence in a way that uses an infinitive. Don't change the meaning of the original sentence.

Example: Rollerskating takes a good sense of balance.

It takes a good sense of balance to rollerskate.

1. Correcting your own bad habits can be very hard.

   _____

2. Walking with a rock in your shoe is painful.

   _____

3. Understanding other cultures is sometimes difficult.

   _____

4. Getting to the concert early was smart.

   _____

5. Traveling in foreign countries is very exciting.

   _____

6. Waking up in a tent in the mountains is a great feeling.

   _____

7. Getting a master's degree will take me two years.

   _____

8. Watching television all day is pretty boring.

   _____

9. Seeing people go hungry is very sad.

   _____

10. Is copying my roommate's homework wrong?

   _____

EXERCISE 3 Change the gerund subject to an infinitive subject.

Example: Renting a car is expensive. *It's expensive to rent a car.*

1. Driving at night is dangerous. _____

2. Completing school without a computer is difficult. _____

3. Staying at home Saturday night isn't fun. _____

PRACTICE **55** Infinitives after Adjectives

EXAMPLE	EXPLANATION
I'm embarrassed **to go** to the party in this old dress. He was surprised **to get** a call from her.	Some adjectives can be followed by an infinitive.

LANGUAGE NOTE:
Some adjectives are often followed by an infinitive:

afraid	glad	relieved
ashamed	happy	sad
disappointed	lucky	sorry
embarrassed	proud	surprised
ready	upset	

EXERCISE 1 Circle the best verb *be* + adjective to complete the sentence.

Example: Are you (ready) / proud to leave for the airport?

1. He <u>was sorry / was glad</u> to see his low grade on the exam.

2. They <u>were embarrassed / were upset</u> to hear of their friend's accident.

3. Some people <u>is afraid / are afraid</u> to go outside after dark.

4. She <u>was happy / was disappointed</u> to learn that her car wasn't going to cost much.

5. I was so <u>sorry / proud</u> to hear the good news about you.

6. We were <u>upset / lucky</u> to get a taxi in this terrible rainstorm.

7. Everyone was <u>surprised / ready</u> to hear of the death of their country's beloved leader.

8. It was no trouble at all. We <u>are afraid / are glad</u> to help you.

9. They are <u>ashamed / lucky</u> to be able to afford a nice house and a reliable car.

10. You should be <u>proud / ashamed</u> to waste all that food.

11. They were <u>sorry / proud</u> to watch their daughter receive the first prize.

12. She was <u>upset / relieved</u> to hear that her baby was healthy.

13. I forgot about the exam. I am <u>ready / surprised</u> to take it today.

14. My family was <u>ready / sad</u> to leave on vacation.

15. Our neighbors were <u>proud / ashamed</u> to show us their flower garden.

16. The police were <u>ready / upset</u> to help people in a car accident.

17. The teenagers were <u>disappointed / embarrassed</u> to receive kisses from their mother.

18. His sister was <u>ready / afraid</u> to walk alone at night.

EXERCISE 2 Complete each of the sentences below with an infinitive.

Example: Parents are always sad _to see their children suffer._

1. Parents are proud _____

2. Students are lucky _____

3. Mice are afraid _____

4. Ducks are glad _____

5. Dogs are happy _____

6. Climbers are relieved _____

7. Teenagers are embarrassed _____

8. I am glad _____

9. I will be glad _____

10. I am disappointed _____

11. I am embarrassed _____

12. I am ready _____

13. I will be sorry _____

14. My friend was upset _____

15. I was prepared _____

EXERCISE 3 Fill in the blank for each of the following with a subject + an appropriate form of the verb *be*.

Examples: _____ She was _____ ashamed to receive poor grades.

_____ I am _____ sorry to hear that you are sick.

1. _____ lucky to have so many wonderful friends.

2. _____ afraid to take the entrance exam for that school.

3. _____ upset to drive her car in a heavy rainstorm last night.

4. _____ afraid to speak on the telephone in English.

5. _____ glad to eat fruit and ice cream for dessert.

6. _____ surprised to receive my letter yesterday in the mail.

7. _____ glad to meet you at the party last week.

8. _____ disappointed to lose your wallet and your money.

PRACTICE **56** Infinitives after Verbs

EXAMPLE	EXPLANATION
Both sides agreed **to end** the war.	Some verbs are commonly followed by an infinitive (phrase).
Some of the soldiers refused **to go** home.	
The people began **to rebuild** their homes.	
Everyone decided **to make** a new start.	

LANGUAGE NOTE:

We can use an infinitive after the following verbs:

agree	forget	prefer
ask	hope	promise
attempt	learn	refuse
begin	like	remember
continue	love	start
decide	need	try
expect	plan	want

EXERCISE 1 Fill in each blank with the infinitive form of a verb from the box.

invade	receive	wait	help	be	destroy
work	send	lose	resist	give	

Example: The soldiers tried _____*to invade*_____ the city, but they couldn't.

1. No one expected the city _____ able to resist their attack.

2. The government hoped _____ more soldiers to defend the city.

3. The enemy forgot _____ the main bridge across the river.

4. The government asked other countries _____.

5. The other countries preferred _____ and see what happened.

6. They promised _____ whatever aid they could.

7. The people didn't want _____ their homes to the enemy.

8. They learned _____ together for the common good.

9. They continued _____ the enemy month after month.

10. They needed _____ fresh supplies of food and arms.

EXERCISE 2 Choose an appropriate verb for each blank. The verbs in the box below may be used more than one time each. Use the correct verb tense.

decide	hope	prefer
continue	refuse	like
ask	promise	want
need	begin	start

Example: At a wedding last week, the bride and groom _____*promised*_____ to love each other.

1. After much discussion, we _____ to talk about the pollution problem.

2. It _____ to rain day after day after day.

3. My parents _____ to retire while they are still healthy and active.

4. The policeman _____ to see the woman's driver's license.

5. She _____ to show it to him.

6. You _____ to tell me what kind of flowers you wanted me to buy.

7. You _____ to write it down.

8. They _____ to take their vacation in the winter.

9. Daddy opened the book and _____ to read to us.

10. It's getting dark in here. We _____ to turn on some lights.

EXERCISE 3 Write an appropriate answer to each question using an infinitive.

1. What was your plan for your future when you were a child?
    I planned to be an astronaut when I grew up.

2. What's an activity that you love to do?
    _____

3. What's something that you need to do this week?
    _____

4. What kind of work do you want to do for a job?
    _____

5. What's something you've tried unsuccessfully to do?
    _____

6. What's something interesting you've begun in the past six months?
    _____

PRACTICE 57 Gerunds or Infinitives after Verbs

EXAMPLE	EXPLANATION
Gerund: I started **looking** for a job a month ago. *Infinitive:* I started **to look** for a job a month ago. *Gerund:* He continued **working** until he was 65. *Infinitive:* He continued **to work** until he was 65.	Some verbs including those listed below can be followed by either a gerund or an infinitive: attempt deserve prefer begin hate start can't stand like try continue love

LANGUAGE NOTE:

Try followed by a gerund is a little different from *try* followed by an infinitive:

Infinitive: I'll try to *improve* my résumé. [*try* = make an effort.]

Gerund: If you can't find a job by looking at the want ads, you should try *networking*. [*try* = use a different technique]

EXERCISE 1 Change the infinitive to a gerund or the gerund to an infinitive in each of the following statements. Pay attention to verb tenses.

Example: I started working at the fast-food restaurant last week.

I started to work at the fast-food restaurant last week.

1. He attempted to find a new job in the newspaper.

   _____

2. All children deserve someone looking after them.

   _____

3. I prefer swimming in lakes to the ocean.

   _____

4. She began to work at a store when she was 16 years old.

   _____

5. We hate worrying about our children's safety.

   _____

6. The parents started to form a group to talk to the teachers.

   _____

7. You can't stand eating red meat.

   _____

8. I liked talking to my friends after high school every day.

   _____

9. The man tried to help the people who were lost.

    _____

10. The women continue to volunteer for the library.

    _____

11. Most cats can't stand to bathe in water.

    _____

12. We love visiting our aunt and uncle.

    _____

13. They deserved winning the writing prize.

    _____

14. It begins getting colder this time of year.

    _____

EXERCISE 2 Fill in each blank with either the infinitive or gerund form of the verbs in parentheses.

Example: I wish you would remember (infinitive—take) _____*to take*_____ off your

shoes before you come into the house.

1. Try (gerund—learn) _____ at least 10 new vocabulary words
    every day.

2. People who have trouble getting to sleep should try (gerund—read)
    _____ in bed.

3. We tried (infinitive—push) _____ the car out of the road, but it was
    just too heavy.

4. The plants will die if you don't start (infinitive—water) _____ them.

5. Did you attempt (gerund—close) _____ the windows before you left
    the house?

6. I love (infinitive—walk) _____ in the woods in fall.

PRACTICE 58 Infinitives to Show Purpose

EXAMPLE	EXPLANATION
You can use the Internet **to get** job information.	We use the infinitive to show the purpose of an action. We can also say *in order to*:
He's working hard and saving his money **to buy** a house.	I am saving my money **in order to buy** a house.

EXERCISE 1 Unscramble the words to write correct statements and questions.

Example: to pay / to sell / I / my plane ticket / had / for / my textbooks/ in order

I had to sell my textbooks in order to pay for my plane ticket.

1. my pronunciation / the best way / what is / to improve

_____?

2. in the paper / she / a new roommate / an ad / to find / put

_____.

3. had / here / to take / we / three buses / to get / in order

_____.

4. weight / in order/ should / what / do / to lose / I

_____?

5. these / your arms / to strengthen / you / should / do / exercises

_____.

6. with your teacher / an appointment / to review / make / your examination

_____.

7. 10 words / to build / every day / you / can / your vocabulary / in order / learn

_____.

EXERCISE 2 Complete each sentence with an infinitive to show purpose. Choose infinitives from the box to help with the answer.

to dispose of	to keep	to cut	to buy	to type
to clean	to buy	to call	to research	to find
to look up	to cool off	to show		

Example: People use a dictionary

People use a dictionary to look up the meanings of words.

1. People use a refrigerator

   _____

2. People use money

   _____

3. Travelers use passports

   _____

4. People who are eating use knives

   _____

5. People use telephones

   _____

6. People use toothbrushes

   _____

7. Students use computers

   _____

8. Travelers use maps

   _____

9. Shoppers use credit cards

   _____

10. People use libraries

    _____

11. People use trash cans

    _____

12. People use air conditioners

    _____

EXERCISE 3 Answer each question about yourself on the lines below.

Example: What do you listen to music for?

I listen to music in order to relax.

1. What do you do in order to relax?

   _____

2. What will you use your education for?

   _____

PRACTICE 59 Overview of Adjective Clauses

EXAMPLE	EXPLANATION
She'd like to marry a man **who knows how to cook.** She'd like to have a job **that uses her talents.** The man **whom you married** is very responsible. The job **that I have** gives me a lot of satisfaction.	An adjective clause is a group of words that describes a noun. It follows the noun. Relative pronouns introduce an adjective clause: *who(m)* for people, *which* for things, *that* for people and things.

EXERCISE 1 Match each of the following parts to make 10 logical definitions.

~~Breakfast is~~	a situation	that fall from the sky.
Ink is	people	who has to work for no pay.
A rug is	a dessert	~~that people eat in the morning~~
Firefighters are	ice crystals	that protects the floor.
A war is	~~the meal~~	that goes in our pens.
Trash is	a piece of equipment	in which two sides are in conflict.
A slave is	a liquid	that children love.
Ice cream is	a piece of cloth or skin	that takes pictures.
A camera is	anything	that people throw away.
Snow is	a person	who put out fires.

Example: *Breakfast is the meal that people eat in the morning.*

2. _____

3. _____

4. _____

5. _____

6. _____

7. _____

8. _____

9. _____

10. _____

EXERCISE 2 Fill in each blank with *who*, *that*, or *which*.

Example: This is the story of a man _____who_____ lost a key.

1. The maid _____ found the key was cleaning the room.
2. The key _____ she found had some words on it.
3. The maid threw the key _____ she found into the garbage can.
4. The trash collector found the key _____ the maid threw away.
5. The trash collector _____ worked at the hotel read the words on the key.
6. The trash collector cleaned the key _____ he found.
7. The trash collector _____ was curious put the key in a bag.
8. The trash collector took the key to a shopkeeper _____ worked next door.
9. The shopkeeper _____ thanked the man identified the key.
10. The shopkeeper paid $100 to the trash collector _____ found the key in the garbage can.
11. The shopkeeper used the key _____ opened a safe.
12. The key opened the safe _____ contained many diamond rings.

EXERCISE 3 Circle the noun that the adjective clause describes. Underline the adjective clause.

Example: I enjoy (movies) that have happy endings.

1. I like people who have nice smiles.
2. He enjoys music that helps him relax.
3. We like to relax in places that are near the ocean.
4. They want to know college students who like to travel.
5. I chose the black skirt that makes me look thin.
6. You look at magazines that are about the world news.
7. I want to own a car that looks adventurous.
8. She wants to marry a man who will always be kind and good.
9. We need to take courses that will improve our job skills.
10. I'd like to live in a house that has three bedrooms.

PRACTICE 60 Relative Pronouns as Subjects

A relative pronoun can be the subject of the adjective clause.

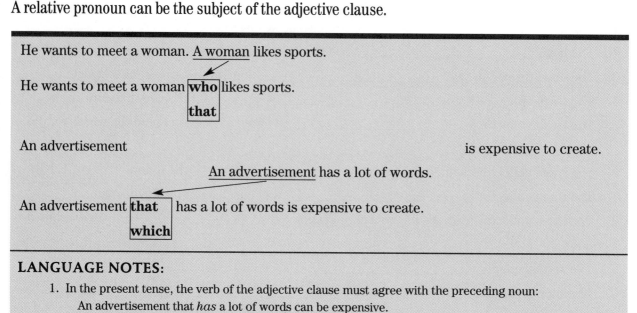

He wants to meet a woman. A woman likes sports.

He wants to meet a woman who likes sports.
that

An advertisement   is expensive to create.

An advertisement has a lot of words.

An advertisement that has a lot of words is expensive to create.
which

LANGUAGE NOTES:

1. In the present tense, the verb of the adjective clause must agree with the preceding noun:
   An advertisement that *has* a lot of words can be expensive.
   Advertisements that *have* a lot of words can be expensive.
2. *Who* and *that* of an adjective clause can contract with *is.*
   He's looking for a woman *who's* smarter than he is.

EXERCISE 1 Circle the correct form of the verb from the underlined verbs in the adjective clause.

Example: I know a girl who (comes)/ come from Somalia.

1. What's the name of the person who is / are singing that song?

2. He wants to marry someone who understand / understands him well.

3. We welcome everyone who come / comes here.

4. She'll have to borrow the money that is / are needed.

5. Will the person who has / have my notebook please return it?

6. She ate the rest of the cookies that was / were in the box.

7. The lady who work / works in the book department will give you a receipt.

8. Could you bring us some of the fruit that grow / grows on your apple tree?

9. I bought pens that don't / doesn't write well.

10. I really don't like sports that is / are violent.

Unscramble the words in each sentence to make a correct statement with an adjective clause.

Example: love/ I / kind to me / the aunt / was / who

I love the aunt who was kind to me.

1. the man / to play / taught / that's / the flute / who / me

   _____ .

2. which / the car / was / bought / old and ugly / we

   _____ .

3. painted / who / who / that famous picture / the artist / was

   _____ ?

4. get / are / people / upset / very sensitive / easily / who / there

   _____ .

5. today / this / came / is / the mail / that

   _____ ?

6. which / we / on the first / must / pay / of the month / are due / the bills

   _____ .

7. a friend / have / you / can help / do / who / me

   _____ ?

8. that / the most options / the computer / prefer / has / I

   _____ .

9. dropped / where / who / is / this wallet / the person

   _____ ?

10. buy / works / let's / better / than this one / an umbrella / that

    _____ .

PRACTICE 61 Relative Pronouns as Objects

A relative pronoun can be the object of the adjective clause.

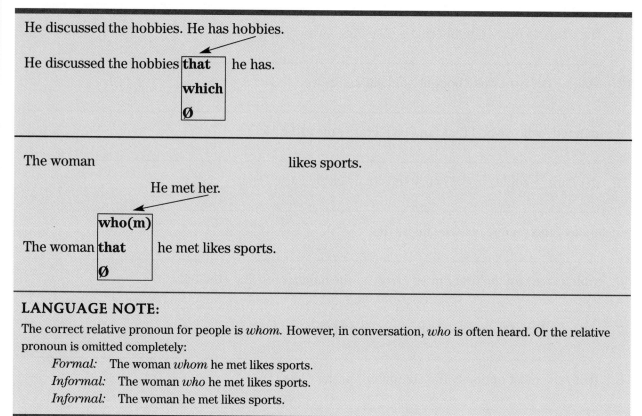

He discussed the hobbies. He has hobbies.

He discussed the hobbies **that / which / Ø** he has.

The woman likes sports.

He met her.

The woman **who(m) / that / Ø** he met likes sports.

LANGUAGE NOTE:

The correct relative pronoun for people is *whom*. However, in conversation, *who* is often heard. Or the relative pronoun is omitted completely:

Formal: The woman *whom* he met likes sports.
Informal: The woman *who* he met likes sports.
Informal: The woman he met likes sports.

EXERCISE 1 Fill in each blank with who*(m)*, or *which*. Do not use *that* in this exercise.

Example: The politician _____who_____ we met was very friendly.

1. I got tickets to the concert _____ you told me about.

2. The movie _____ we saw yesterday was excellent.

3. There goes the person _____ I'm going to marry.

4. The envelope _____ you sent me had nothing in it.

5. The woman _____ you spoke to was my mother.

6. I liked the book _____ you gave me.

7. I have friends _____ like to get together whenever possible.

8. The doctor said to avoid foods _____ have a high sugar content.

9. I like a man _____ knows what he wants.

10. The food _____ we ate was very spicy.

EXERCISE **2** Underline the adjective clause in each sentence. Then cross out the relative pronoun to make each sentence or question informal. Rewrite each sentence with no relative pronoun.

Example: Did you read every book ~~that~~ the teacher assigned?

Informal: Did you read every book the teacher assigned?

1. I like the people that I met yesterday.

   Informal: _____

2. The pizza that I ate didn't agree with me.

   Informal: _____

3. This is the man whom I spoke of last week.

   Informal: _____

4. The reason that you gave was not a good enough one.

   Informal: _____

5. Spring is the season that I like best.

   Informal: _____

6. The teacher that I wanted to speak to was on vacation.

   Informal: _____

7. What did you say to the girl whom I met yesterday?

   Informal: _____

8. The music that he played was too loud.

   Informal: _____

9. I waited all day for the repairman that you recommended.

   Informal: _____

10. The soccer games that we played in high school were always exciting.

    Informal: _____

11. I enjoyed reading the book that you recommended.

    Informal: _____

12. He got that camera from the man whom I told you about.

    Informal: _____

PRACTICE 62 Comparative and Superlative Forms

	SIMPLE	COMPARATIVE	SUPERLATIVE
One-syllable adjectives and adverbs	tall	taller	the tallest
Two-syllable adjectives that end in –y	easy	easier	easiest
Other two-syllable adjectives	frequent	more frequent	the most frequent
Some two-syllable adjectives have two forms.	simple	simpler more simple	the simplest the most simple

Note: These two-syllable adjectives have two forms: *common, handsome, quiet, gentle, narrow, clever, friendly, angry.*

	SIMPLE	COMPARATIVE	SUPERLATIVE
Adjectives with three or more syllables	important	more important	the most important
–ly adverbs	quickly	more quickly	the most quickly
Irregular adjectives and adverbs	good / well bad / badly far little a lot	better worse farther / further less more	the best the worst the farthest / furthest the least the most

Note: Farther is used for distances. Further is used for ideas.

LANGUAGE NOTES:

1. Most adjectives that end in –ed and –ing use *more* and *the most*, not –er or –est:
    more tired   most disturbing
2. The comparative form compares two similar things, using *than*. The superlative form compares one thing to two or more other similar things:
    Comparative: The blue car is faster *than* the red car.
    Superlative: That ring is the most beautiful of those five rings.

EXERCISE 1 Choose the correct form of the adjective.

Example: That is the <u>more ugly</u> / (ugliest) dog that I have ever seen.

1. This has been the <u>wonderfulest / most wonderful</u> evening of my life.
2. I like to buy pants that are a little <u>tighter / more tight</u> than these.
3. I ate two sandwiches, but my little brother was <u>hungrier / more hungry</u> and he ate three.
4. They were the <u>deliciousest / most delicious</u> sandwiches I'd ever eaten.
5. Don't be so rude. Try to ask <u>politer / more polite</u> questions.
6. She's too nervous for this job. We need someone <u>calmer / more calm</u>.
7. You're the <u>interestingest / most interesting</u> person I've met here.
8. Hawaii is a much <u>wetter / more wet</u> place than Arizona.
9. As she grew older, she became <u>beautifuller / more beautiful</u>.

10. You need to get here earlier / more early if you want the best bargains.

11. No farther / further meetings have been scheduled.

12. I'm sorry, I don't understand. Could you repeat that slowlier / more slowly?

EXERCISE 2 Choose the simple, the comparative, or the superlative form.

Example: This test is important / more important / (the most important) of all the tests.

1. That was a very rough / rougher / roughest airplane flight.

2. She's good / better / the best than most people at learning languages.

3. I'm afraid that I did really badly / worse / the worst on that exam.

4. Many Americans think that Abraham Lincoln was the great / greater / greatest American president of all.

5. What a waste of money! This new clock radio is absolutely useless / more useless / the most useless.

6. The hot / hotter / hottest place in the world is in Mauritania.

7. This trip has been long / longer / the longest than I expected it to be.

8. Every night you come home late / later / the latest than the night before.

9. Is it true that Athens is the noisy /noisier /noisiest city in the world?

10. Some people are friendly / friendlier / the friendliest than others.

11. I want to buy a pretty / prettier / the prettiest dress.

12. She lost the lottery last time, but this time she was lucky / luckier / the luckiest.

EXERCISE 3 Answer each question using a superlative or comparative adjective.

1. Who is the nicest person you know?

   _____

2. Is a grammar test or a bad cold worse?

   _____

PRACTICE 63 Superlatives

EXAMPLE	EXPLANATION
Michael Jordan was the most popular basketball player of his time.	We use the superlative form to point out the number 1 item of a group of two or more.
He became one of the richest people in the world.	
For many years, he was the most valuable player.	

LANGUAGE NOTES:

1. Use *the* before a superlative form. Omit *the* if there is a possessive form before the superlative form.
   Jack is *my* tallest friend.
2. We sometimes put a prepositional phrase at the end of a superlative sentence:
   in the world   in my family   in my class   in my country
3. We sometimes say "*one of the*" before a superlative form. Then we use a plural noun.
   He was *one of the best athletes* in the world.
4. An adjective clause with *ever* and the present perfect tense often completes a superlative statement:
   Jordan is one of the best athletes *who has ever lived*.

EXERCISE 1   Complete each statement with a superlative adjective from the box.

easiest	wisest	rarest	largest	fastest
worst	silliest	shortest	greatest	smallest

Example: The Sears Tower is one of the world's _____*tallest*_____ buildings.

1. Gandhi was one of the _____ people who ever lived.
2. The tiger is one of the _____ animals in the world.
3. February is the _____ month in the year.
4. Jupiter is the _____ of all the planets.
5. Monaco is one of the _____ countries in the world.
6. Comedies can be the _____ kinds of movies.
7. Picasso was one of the _____ painters of his time.
8. The cheetah is the _____ animal on four legs.
9. The mosquito is one of the _____ insects.
10. E-mail is one of the _____ forms of communication.

EXERCISE 2 Answer each of the following questions with a complete sentence.

Example: **Q:** What is the most beautiful city in your country?

A: _I think Madrid is the most beautiful city in my country._

1. **Q:** Who is the most powerful leader in your country?
   A: _____

2. **Q:** Who is one of the most popular singers in your country?
   A: _____

3. **Q:** What animal do you think is the most intelligent?
   A: _____

4. **Q:** What is your hardest subject in school?
   A: _____

5. **Q:** When did you meet your best friend?
   A: _____

6. **Q:** Who is one of the happiest people that you know?
   A: _____

7. **Q:** What was one of the most important inventions of the twentieth century?
   A: _____

8. **Q:** What time does your earliest class start?
   A: _____

9. **Q:** Who is one of the most famous people in the world?
   A: _____

10. **Q:** What is the saddest movie that you've ever seen?
    A: _____.

PRACTICE 64 Equality and Difference with Nouns and Adjectives

NOUN	ADJECTIVE	EXAMPLE
height	tall, short	He's **the same height as** his wife. He's **as tall as** his wife. He's *not* **the same (height) as** his brother. His brother is **shorter.**
age	old, young	He's **the same age as** his cousin. He's **as old as** his cousin. He's *not* **the same (age) as** his wife. His wife is **older.**
weight	heavy, thin	She's **the same weight as** her sister. She's **as heavy as** her sister. She's *not* **the same (weight) as** her mother. She is **thinner.**
length	long, short	This shelf is **the same length as** the couch. This shelf is **as long as** the couch. This shelf is *not* **the same (length) as** that room. This shelf is **shorter.**
price	expensive, cheap	This car is **the same price as** that car. This car is **as expensive as** that car. This car is *not* **the same (price) as** that car. This car is **cheaper.**
size	big, small	These shoes are **the same size as** those sneakers. These shoes are **as big as** those sneakers. These shoes are *not* **the same (size) as** those shoes. These shoes are **smaller.**

LANGUAGE NOTES:

1. For equality with nouns, use *the same . . . as:*
   She's *the same age as* her husband.
2. For equality with adjectives and adverbs, use *as . . . as:*
   She's *as old as* her husband.
3. For difference with nouns, use *not the same as:*
   She's *not the same age as* her sister.   She and her sister are *not the same age.*
4. For difference with adjectives, use *(different) from:*
   She's *taller than* her brother.   She's *different from* her brother.

EXERCISE 1 Fill in each blank with a noun from the box.

height	age	weight	length	price	size

Example: A meter is about the same ___*length*___ as a yard.

1. Your new sport utility vehicle is almost the same _____ as your apartment!

2. She has a teacher who is the same _____ as her father.

3. Do you have a better computer that's about the same _____ as this one?

4. Is a liter about the same _____ as a quart?

5. You're growing so fast that now you're the same _____ as your older sister.

6. I think the used car I bought was the same _____ as the last new one I bought.

7. I'm so tired. Is your backpack the same _____ as mine?

8. I need a box that's about the same _____ as this gift so that I can mail it.

EXERCISE 2 Read each sentence, and then write a second sentence that means the same thing, using *not as . . . as.*

Example: The highway is wider than the road.

The road isn't as wide as the highway. _____

1. The Netherlands is flatter than Switzerland.

   _____

2. Switzerland is more mountainous than the Netherlands.

   _____

3. He's friendlier than his roommate.

   _____

4. The Himalayas are taller than the Alps.

   _____

5. This movie was more interesting than the last one we saw.

   _____

6. A dog is easier to train than a cat.

   _____

7. Your teacher is more helpful than mine.

   _____

8. Baseball is slower than soccer.

   _____

PRACTICE 65 Overview of the Passive Voice

EXAMPLE	EXPLANATION
The fire **was started** by a careless camper.	The passive verb uses a form of *be* + the past participle.
Many trees **were burned** down.	The passive voice is used when the subject receives the action of the verb.
The fire **will be put out** by the Forest Service.	Sometimes the performer of the action is included after a passive verb. Use *by* + noun or object pronoun before the performer.
Some homes **were burned.**	Usually a performer is not included in a passive sentence

LANGUAGE NOTE:
The verb in passive voice shows that the subject receives the action. The verb in active voice shows that the subject performs the action of the verb. Compare:

Active: The cat ate the mouse. ⟶ Passive: The mouse was eaten by the cat.

EXERCISE 1 Underline the verb in each sentence. Identify each sentence as passive or active.

Examples: My best friend just *sent* me some great news by e-mail.   _____*active*_____

Our friend Kathy *may not be accepted* to the university.   _____*passive*_____

1. Radium was discovered by Marie Curie.   _____

2. Jesse is finishing up the project right now.   _____

3. His parents have sent him two packages this month.   _____

4. You ought to be examined by a specialist.   _____

5. The stock market has been climbing steadily for the past six weeks.

_____

6. These beautiful carpets are made entirely by hand.   _____

7. The new subway is being constructed by the McArthur Company.

_____

8. The winners of the Nobel Prizes will be announced by the Nobel Committee later this week.

_____

9. This birthday cake was baked by my roommate.   _____

10. Why did he give you such an ugly look?   _____

11. This window must have been broken by a baseball.   _____

12. We'll have to replace it.   _____

13. The children have been told by their parents not to play ball near the house.

    _____

14. The window ought to be paid for by them. _____

15. Everyone enjoyed the camping trip. _____

16. One of the pieces of the puzzle was lost. _____

17. I cook breakfast for my family every morning. _____

18. Corn is grown in Kansas. _____

EXERCISE 2 Choose the correctly formed passive verb to complete each sentence.

Example: Tonight's news sponsers /(is sponsored) by the ACME Corporation.

1. The First National Bank was robbed / robbed today around 5:00 p.m.

2. The robbers has not been caught / have not been caught yet.

3. Six firefighters were taked / were taken out of a forest fire 50 miles east of here.

4. They were brought / were brung to the hospital for second-degree burns.

5. All roads in the area has been closed / have been closed to everyone except the firefighters.

6. A new mayor elected / was elected.

7. Results of the election were announced / was announced just an hour ago.

8. A conference on disease is being hold / is being held this week at the Medical Center.

9. A new drug to fight the disease have been study / has been studied by researchers at our medical school.

10. The research project was starting / was started by a group of international corporations.

EXERCISE 3 Underline the passive verb. Write who did the action at the end of each statement.

Example: The door was opened _____*by the wind.*_____

1. The cat was fed _____

2. Children are raised _____

3. The composition was typed _____

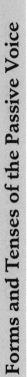

PRACTICE **66** Forms and Tenses of the Passive Voice

TENSE	ACTIVE	PASSIVE (*BE* + PAST PARTICIPLE)
Simple Present	They **take a** vote.	A vote is **taken.**
Simple Past	They **took** a vote.	A vote **was taken.**
Future	They **will take** a vote.	A vote **will be taken.**
	They **are going to take** a vote.	A vote **is going to be taken.**
Present Perfect	They **have taken** a vote.	A vote **has been taken.**
Modal	They **must take** a vote.	A vote **must be taken.**

LANGUAGE NOTE:

The passive voice can be used with different tenses and with modals. The past participle remains the same for every tense. Only the form of *be* changes.

EXERCISE 1 Change each of the following sentences from active to passive. Do not include a performer. (Do not include *by* + the performer.)

Examples: They could build a new house. *A new house could be built.*

She drank orange juice. *Orange juice was drunk.*

1. They planned it carefully.

   _____

2. She threw the ball.

   _____

3. When will you finish your composition?

   _____

4. You should send the letter.

   _____

5. I can't change the tire here.

   _____

6. They bought the T-shirt at the fair.

   _____

7. We are going to paint the house.

   _____

8. We didn't eat the pie.

   _____

EXERCISE 2 Change each of the following sentences from passive to active.

Example: Their old house was built in 1930 by her grandfather.

Her grandfather _built their old house in 1930._____

1. The new house is being built by the Johnson Brothers.

   The Johnson Brothers _____

2. The plans for the new garden haven't been completed yet.

   They _____

3. Trees, flowers, and grass will have to be planted after the house is completed.

   They _____

4. The bank loan must be repaid within 30 years.

   They _____

5. The loan for the old house had been paid off just a few years ago.

   They _____

6. The new house was designed by their oldest daughter.

   Their oldest daughter _____

7. The house will be painted by the family.

   The family _____

8. The students should be shown examples by the teacher.

   The teacher _____

EXERCISE 3 Write a passive sentence for each of the following subjects.

Example: The Eiffel Tower _was built in Paris in the nineteenth century._____

1. The cat _____

2. The grades _____

3. The food _____

4. The car _____

5. The computer _____

6. The train _____

PRACTICE 67 Classifying or Identifying the Subject with the Indefinite Article

EXAMPLE	EXPLANATION
A tent is **a** shelter that is used by campers. Electricity was **an** important invention. My brother is **a** forest ranger.	We use the indefinite articles *a* and *an* to classify or define the subject of a sentence.
Passports are official documents used by travelers. My parents are bank workers.	When we classify a plural subject, we don't use any article at all.

LANGUAGE NOTE:

When we classify or identify the subject, we are telling who or what the subject is:

What is a hammer?   A hammer is a tool.
Who was Albert Einstein?   He was a great physicist.

EXERCISE 1   Match each question with its answer.

1. Dew is _____d_____
2. A watch is _____
3. A map is _____
4. Pineapples are _____
5. Farmers are _____
6. An alarm is _____
7. Tourists are _____
8. A lifeguard is _____
9. Forest rangers are _____
10. A ruler is _____

a. a device that sounds a warning.
b. a device for measuring things.
c. people who take care of forests.
d. water on the grass in the morning.
e. a drawing that shows where things are.
f. vacationers who are sightseeing.
g. a person who saves swimmers in danger.
h. people who grow crops to sell them.
i. a device that tells time.
j. tropical fruit.

EXERCISE 2   Correct each of the following sentences by adding *a* or *an* in the sentence where they are needed.

Example: Omelet is dish made with eggs.

An omelet is a dish made with eggs.

1. Bird is animal that flies and lays eggs.

_____

2. Gasoline is fuel that is made from petroleum.

_____

3. Train is form of public transportation.

_____

4. Trail is small path that is used by hikers.

_____

5. Match is small stick of wood or paper that is used to start fire.

_____

6. Stove is appliance that is used to cook food in kitchen.

_____

7. Kitchen is room where people prepare their food.

_____

8. Ice cream is frozen dessert that is made from cream, sugar, and flavorings.

_____

9. Glue is liquid that is used to stick things together.

_____

10. Ring is round piece of metal that is worn on finger.

_____

11. Wedding ring is ring that is used to show that someone is married.

_____

12. Workbook is book that is filled with exercises.

_____

13. Scanner is electronic device that can copy pictures and words.

_____

EXERCISE 3 Write a sentence that classifies, identifies, or defines the words below. Use the proper form of the verb *be*.

Example: A tablecloth _is a cloth that is used to cover a table._

1. A door _____

2. A planet _____

3. Volcanoes _____

4. Pets _____

5. A truck _____

68 Introducing a Noun with the Indefinite Article

	SINGULAR COUNT	PLURAL COUNT	NONCOUNT
Affirmative	We need **a** new tent. I'm taking **an** umbrella.	We'll need **(some)** matches.	Let's take **(some)** drinking water.
Negative	Don't bring **a** hair dryer.	We won't need **(any)** electric devices.	We don't have **(any)** ice.
Question	Will there be **a** picnic table?	Did you pack **(any)** cups and plates?	Will there be **(any)** firewood for sale?

LANGUAGE NOTES:

1. We use *a* or *an* to introduce a singular noun into the conversation. We use *some* or *any* to introduce a noncount noun or a plural noun into the conversation:

2. *Some* and *any* can be omitted:

   I don't have *any* time to help you.

   I don't have time to help you.

EXERCISE 1 Complete each sentence with *a, an, any,* or *some.*

Example: Do you want _____*a*_____ donut?

1. Do you have _____ sugar I could borrow?

2. He will need _____ new notebook for his new class.

3. She was buying _____ beautiful ceramic vase at the store

4. We don't buy _____ artwork until the bills are paid.

5. _____ people have moved to Costa Rica recently.

6. Your teacher won't teach _____ pronunciation course next semester.

7. The children want _____ lemonade. They are thirsty.

8. My family rode to _____ wonderful restaurant.

9. The car doesn't have _____ gas right now. Sorry.

10. Did he carry _____ toothpaste in his bag?

11. Did she take _____ pictures at her class reunion?

12. _____ picnic is _____ outdoor meal.

13. _____ bird doesn't have _____ teeth, so it never needs _____ dentist.

14. I'm making _____ cake and _____ cookies for my son's party.

Answer each of the questions completely. Use *a*, *an*, *any* and *some*.

Example:

    Q: What's something that people sometimes drink in the morning to give them vitamins?

    A: *People sometimes drink some orange juice in the morning to get some vitamins.*

1. **Q:** What is something you can't take on an airplane?

    A: _____

    _____

2. **Q:** What should you not forget to take on a car trip?

    A: _____

    _____

3. **Q:** What should you take when you go shopping?

    A: _____

    _____

4. **Q:** What do you always keep in your refrigerator?

    A: _____

    _____

5. **Q:** What do you usually eat for breakfast?

    A: _____

    _____

6. **Q:** What did you buy the last time you went to a grocery store?

    A: _____

    _____

7. **Q:** What do you need to bring to class?

    A: _____

    _____

8. **Q:** What is needed to make a cake?

    A: _____

Introducing a Noun with the Indefinite Article

PRACTICE 69 The Definite Article

EXAMPLE	EXPLANATION
The bank gives you *a personal identification number.* You should memorize **the** number.	A noun is first introduced as an indefinite noun. When referring to it again, the definite article *the* is used.
Would you please get **the** milk out of **the** refrigerator?	The speaker is referring to a person or an object that is present.
The sun is not very bright in the winter. There are many problems in **the** world.	There is only one in our experience.
Where's **the** teacher? I have a question about **the** homework.	The speaker and the listener share a common experience. Students in the same class talk about **the** teacher, **the** homework, **the** chalkboard.
I spent **the** money you gave me.	The speaker defines or specifies exactly which one.
I went to **the** store for some groceries. I stopped by **the** bank to get some cash.	We often use *the* with certain familiar places and people when we refer to the one that we usually use: the bank the beach the bus the zoo the post office the train the park the doctor the store

LANGUAGE NOTE:

We use the definite article *the* when the speaker and the listener have the same person(s) or objects(s) in mind. The listener knows exactly what the speaker is referring to as in the examples above.

EXERCISE 1 Read the following paragraph. Then fill in each blank with *a, an,* or *the.*

Yesterday I decided to find (**Example**) _____*an*_____ apartment to rent. So I bought (1)

_____ newspaper and found (2) _____ advertisement for (3)

_____ one-bedroom apartment that sounded perfect for me. I called (4)

_____ number printed in the paper. (5) _____ landlord answered, and he

told me about (6) _____ apartment. Today I met (7) _____ landlord at

(8) _____ apartment so that I could have a look at it. I liked (9) _____ living

room, but (10) _____ bedroom was a little small. I decided to take it anyway.

(11) _____ apartment isn't furnished, so I'll have to get some furniture. Fortunately, I already have (12) _____ table and (13) _____ armchair. I will have to buy (14) _____ bed. I don't want to sleep on (15) _____ floor!

EXERCISE 2 Insert *a, an, the, some,* or *any* wherever they are appropriate.

Example: My friends and I took _____*a*_____ vacation. _____*The*_____ vacation was wonderful.

1. It was _____ very quiet place.
2. Every day _____ sun woke us up as it came through _____ eastern window of _____ little cabin that we rented.
3. We made _____ good breakfast and drank _____ good hot tea with it.
4. There wasn't _____ telephone or _____ television in the cabin.
5. For entertainment we took _____ long walks in the countryside.
6. We had _____ good conversations.
7. Every day after lunch we wrote _____ postcards.
8. Then we mailed _____ postcards at _____ post office.
9. In _____ evening we watched _____ moon rise.
10. We looked for _____ first star.
11. We didn't feel _____ tension for _____ whole time that we were there.
12. We still talk about _____ wonderful time that we had together.

EXERCISE 3 Unscramble the words to write correct sentences

Example: a / the / the / map / city / telephone book / find / of / can / you / in

You can find a map of the city in the telephone book.

1. today / a / the / the / is having / on / shop / corner / sale
   _____

2. teacher / we will have /substitute / so / a / teacher / the / is sick today
   _____

3. go to / at / look / zoo / bears / let's / the / the / and
   _____

4. to listen / like / rain / roof / on / the / the / I / to
   _____

5. dictionary / I / need / that I / to replace / lost / the
   _____

Indefinite Pronouns

PRACTICE 70 Indefinite Pronouns

DEFINITE PRONOUN	INDEFINITE PRONOUN
My daughter has a new doll. Do you want to see **it?**	My daughter has a new doll. Her friend has **one** too.
He got money from his grandparents. He wants to spend **it.**	He got money for his birthday. You got **some** too. Did you get **any** for your graduation?
I have a young son. I take **him** to the park every day.	I have a son. Do you have **one?**
My son has some video games. He likes to play with **them.**	My son has some video games. Does your son have **any?**

LANGUAGE NOTES:

1. We use definite pronouns (*him, her, them, it*) to refer to definite count nouns.
2. We use *one* to refer to an indefinite singular count noun.
3. We use *some* (for statements) and *any* (for negatives and questions) to refer to an indefinite noncount noun or an indefinite plural count noun.
4. We can use *any* and *some* before *more*.

EXERCISE 1 Read each sentence. Then fill in the blanks with an indefinite pronoun (*some, any,* or *one*) or a definite pronoun: (*them* and *it*).

Example: I had a VCR, but I spilled _____*the*_____ drink I had on it, and now _____*it*_____ won't work.

1. I need to either get _____ repaired or else buy a new _____.

2. I saw an ad for a used _____ in the campus newspaper.

3. I'm going to go and look at _____ tonight.

4. Maybe my parents will give me _____ for my birthday.

5. They cost a lot of money, and right now I don't have _____.

6. If I got a part-time job, I could earn _____.

7. My neighbor has two. He uses _____ to copy videotapes.

8. Maybe he'd lend me _____ until I can buy _____.

9. I could return _____ to him whenever he needed _____.

10. He had three VCRs, but he gave _____ to his daughter last month.

EXERCISE 2 Answer each question. Substitute the underlined words with an indefinite pronoun (*one, some, any*) or a definite pronoun (*it, them*).

Example: Do you like *horror movies?*

No, I don't like them at all.

1. Do you have a bus pass?

   _____

2. Where do you do your grocery shopping?

   _____

3. How often do you write letters to your family?

   _____

4. Do you have any gum with you?

   _____

5. Does your home have a porch?

   _____

6. Do you have a computer?

   _____

7. Did you buy any CDs this week?

   _____

8. Do you study for exams with your classmates?

   _____

EXERCISE 3 Write a response for each question using *some, any, one, them,* or *it.*

Example: **Q:** Is there a pay phone in this building?

   A: *Yes, there's one next to the elevator.*

1. **Q:** Have you ever ridden a bus in this city?
   A: _____

2. **Q:** Did you have any pets when you were little?
   A: _____

3. **Q:** Did you finish the homework for today?
   A: _____

4. **Q:** Where's the nearest bookstore?
   A: _____

More Grammar Practice 2

Copyright © 2001 by Heinle, a part of the Thomson Corporation. Heinle, Thomson, and the Thomson logo are trademarks used herein under license.

All rights reserved. No part of this work covered by the copyright hereon may be reproduced or used in any form or by any means—graphic, electronic, or mechanical, including photocopying, recording, taping, Web distribution or information storage and retrieval systems—without the written permission of the publisher.

Printed in the United States of America
10   06

For more information contact Heinle, 25 Thomson Place, Boston, Massachusetts 02210 USA, or you can visit our Internet site at http://www.heinle.com

For permission to use material from this text or product contact us:
Tel   1-800-730-2214
Fax   1-800-730-2215
Web   www.thomsonrights.co

ISBN: 0-8384-1902-X
Texas Edition ISBN: 0-8384-5349-X

Printer: *Courier Westford*

International Division List

ASIA (INCLUDING JAPAN AND INDIA)
Thomson Learning
5 Shenton Way #01-01
UIC Building
Singapore 068808

AUSTRALIA/NEW ZEALAND
Thomson Learning
102 Dodds Street
Southbank, Victoria
Australia 3006

CANADA
Thomson Nelson
1120 Birchmount Road
Toronto, Ontario M1K 5G4

LATIN AMERICA
Thomson Learning
Seneca, 53
Colonia Polanco
11560 Mexico D.F. Mexico

SPAIN/PORTUGAL
Thomson Paraninfo
Calle Magallanes, 25
28015 Madrid
Spain

UK/EUROPE/MIDDLE EAST/AFRICA
Thomson Learning
High Holborn House
50/51 Bedford Row
London, WC1R 4LR
United Kingdom